Problem Solving in Mathematics

Grades 3–6

To Barbara for her support, patience, and inspiration.
To my children and grandchildren: David, Lisa, Danny, Max,
Sam, and Jack, whose future is unbounded
And in memory of my dear parents, Ernest and Alice,
who never lost faith in me.

—Alfred S. Posamentier

To my wife and life partner,
Gladys,
who, in her own "efficient" way, develops
"elegant" solutions to the problems I seem to create.

—Stephen Krulik

Problem Solving in Mathematics
Grades 3–6

Powerful Strategies to Deepen Understanding

Alfred S. Posamentier
Stephen Krulik

CORWIN
A SAGE Company

For information:

Corwin
A SAGE Company
2455 Teller Road
Thousand Oaks, California 91320
(800) 233-9936
Fax: (800) 417-2466
www.corwinpress.com

SAGE India Pvt. Ltd.
B 1/I 1 Mohan Cooperative
   Industrial Area
Mathura Road, New Delhi 110 044
India

SAGE Ltd.
1 Oliver's Yard
55 City Road
London EC1Y 1SP
United Kingdom

SAGE Asia-Pacific Pte. Ltd.
33 Pekin Street #02-01
Far East Square
Singapore 048763

Printed in the United States of America

Library of Congress Cataloging-in-Publication Data

Posamentier, Alfred S.
Problem solving in mathematics, grades 3–6: powerful strategies to deepen understanding / Alfred S. Posamentier, Stephen Krulik.
     p. cm.
Includes bibliographical references and index.
ISBN 978-1-4129-6066-3 (cloth)
ISBN 978-1-4129-6067-0 (pbk.)
   1. Problem solving—Study and teaching (Elementary) 2. Mathematics—Study and teaching (Elementary) I. Krulik, Stephen. II. Title.

QA63.P668 2009
372.7—dc22   2008049669

This book is printed on acid-free paper.

09   10   11   12   13   10   9   8   7   6   5   4   3   2   1

Acquisitions Editor:	Cathy Hernandez
Editorial Assistants:	Ena Rosen, Sarah Bartlett
Production Editor:	Cassandra Margaret Seibel
Copy Editor:	Liann Lech
Typesetter:	C&M Digitals (P) Ltd.
Proofreader:	Kevin Gleason
Cover Designers:	Brian Bello, Anthony Paular
Graphic Designer:	Scott Van Atta

Contents

Preface

Over the years, problem solving has emerged as one of the major concerns at all levels of school mathematics. In fact, the National Council of Supervisors of Mathematics (NCSM) points out that "learning to solve problems is the principal reason for studying mathematics" (NCSM 1977, 1). In more recent years, the National Council of Teachers of Mathematics (NCTM), in its *Principles and Standards for School Mathematics*, notes that in the upper elementary grades, "The goal of school mathematics should be for all students to become increasingly able and willing to engage with and solve problems" (NCTM 2000, 182). We are in complete agreement! In fact, we would go one step further—we feel that problem solving is not only a skill to be engaged in mathematics, but also a skill that will be carried over to everyday issues and serve a person well throughout life.

In many cases, students seem to feel that a mathematics problem can be solved in only one way, specific to the *type* of problem being taught (i.e., age problems, motion problems, mixture problems, and so on). Students often feel that some computational procedure or formula is the only approach that will *work*. Where does this misconception come from?

In fact, it is often the teachers themselves who are not aware of the many problem-solving strategies that can be used to provide efficient and elegant solutions to many problems. As Cindy, a prospective elementary school teacher, puts it,

> One thing I realized was that in high school we never learned the theories behind our arithmetic. We just used the formulas and carried out the problem solving. For instance, the way I learned permutations was just to use the factorial of the number and carry out the multiplication. (Ball 1988, 10)

Cindy and her peers unconsciously convey to their students the notion that problems can be solved using only one particular computational approach. Although we would agree that the standard algorithms are powerful tools, unless students can solve problems, such tools are of little use (NCTM 2000). This book is a result of our many years of efforts to make teachers and students aware of this most important aspect of teaching mathematics. The book is designed for the classroom teacher who has a sincere desire to help students succeed as problem solvers both in mathematics and beyond. This is not to say that the book cannot be used by students directly; quite the contrary! However, its *tone* is directed to the teacher, who "can help students become problem solvers by selecting rich and appropriate problems, orchestrating their use, and assessing students' understanding and use of strategies" (NCTM 2000, 185).

In this book, we examine a number of the strategies that are widely used in problem solving, in both mathematics and real-life situations. In the mathematics classroom, these strategies provide an alternate plan for resolving many problem situations that arise within the curriculum. We have selected, within grade bands, several examples to illustrate each strategy, realizing that teachers will wish to apply these strategies to their regular instructional program. To do this, we recommend a careful review and study of the examples provided for each strategy so that the strategy eventually becomes a genuine part of the teacher's thinking processes or, one might say, a part of his or her arsenal of problem-solving tools.

Although it is true that many of these examples can be solved using some formula, such a purely *mechanical* approach often masks some of the efficiency, beauty, and elegance of the mathematics. In many cases, the problem-solving strategies presented make the solution of a problem much easier, much *neater*, much more understandable, and thereby enjoyable!

Throughout the book, we try to show how each of these strategies occurs and ought to be used consciously in real-life situations. Many people already make use of these strategies without realizing it. This carry-over into life outside of the school adds importance to the mathematics our students study and ultimately will improve their everyday performance. We believe that you and your students alike can profit from a careful reading of (and working along with) this book. As you examine each problem, take the time to solve it in any way you wish, or perhaps in a variety of ways. Compare your solutions to those provided. (Naturally, we welcome any clever alternatives to those in the book.) Most importantly, try to absorb the impact of the application of the problem-solving strategies and how they contribute to the beauty and power of mathematics. All the better if you can carry over this motivated feeling to your students.

Understand our feeling that problem solving must be the cornerstone of any successful mathematics program. Then try to infuse this same enthusiastic feeling and attitude in your daily teaching. This concentrated effort will make you a better problem solver and in turn help your students to become better problem solvers also. Not only will their attitude toward mathematics improve, so will their skills and abilities. This is our ultimate goal.

Publisher's Acknowledgments

Corwin gratefully acknowledges the contributions of the following reviewers:

Melinda Jenkins
Elementary Mathematics Specialist
Henrico County Public Schools
Richmond, Virginia

Dr. Timothy J. McNamara
Educational Consultant and Professional Developer
Webster, New York

Janice L. Richardson
Director of Elon Teaching Fellows
Associate Professor and Education Coordinator
Department of Mathematics
Elon University
Elon, North Carolina

Pearl Solomon
Professor Emerita of Teacher Education
St. Thomas Aquinas College
Chestnut Ridge, New York

About the Authors

Alfred S. Posamentier is Dean of the School of Education and Professor of Mathematics Education at The City College of the City University of New York (CCNY). He is the author and co-author of more than 45 mathematics books for teachers, secondary and elementary school students, and the general readership. Dr. Posamentier is also a frequent commentator in newspapers on topics relating to education.

After completing his BA degree in mathematics at Hunter College of the City University of New York, he took a position as a teacher of mathematics at Theodore Roosevelt High School (Bronx, New York), where he focused his attention on improving the students' problem-solving skills and at the same time enriching their instruction far beyond what the traditional textbooks offered. He also developed the school's first mathematics teams (at both the junior and senior level). He is still involved in working with mathematics teachers and supervisors, nationally and internationally, to help them maximize their effectiveness. As dean of the CCNY School of Education, his scope of interest covers the full gamut of educational issues.

Immediately upon joining the CCNY faculty in 1970 (after having received his master's degree there in 1966), he began to develop new in-service courses for secondary school mathematics teachers in such special areas as recreational mathematics and problem solving in mathematics.

In 1973, Dr. Posamentier received his PhD from Fordham University (New York) in mathematics education and has since extended his reputation in mathematics education to Europe. He has been visiting professor at several European universities in Austria, England, Germany, and Poland; while at the University of Vienna, he was Fulbright Professor (1990).

In 1989, he was awarded an Honorary Fellow at the South Bank University (London, England). In recognition of his outstanding teaching, the CCNY Alumni Association named him Educator of the Year in 1994, and New York City had the day, May 1, 1994, named in his honor by the President of the New York City Council. In 1994, he was also awarded the Grand Medal of Honor from the Republic of Austria, and in 1999, upon approval of Parliament, the President of the Republic of Austria awarded him the title of University Professor of Austria. In 2003, he was awarded the title of Ehrenbürger (Honorary Fellow) of the Vienna University of Technology, and in 2004 was awarded the Austrian Cross of Honor for Arts and Science, First Class from the President of the Republic of Austria. In 2005, he was inducted into the Hunter College Alumni Hall of Fame, and in 2006, he was awarded the Townsend Harris Medal by the CCNY Alumni Association.

He has taken on numerous important leadership positions in mathematics education locally. He was a member of the New York State Education Commissioner's Blue Ribbon Panel on the Math-A Regents Exams, as well as the Commissioner's Mathematics Standards Committee, which redefined the standards for New York State, and he also serves on the New York City schools' Chancellor's Math Advisory Panel.

Now in his 39th year on the faculty of the CCNY, he is still a leading commentator on educational issues and continues his long-time passion of seeking ways to make mathematics interesting to teachers, students, and the general public—as can be seen from some of his more recent books from among the more than 45 he has written: *The Art of Problem Solving: A Resource for the Mathematics Teacher* (Corwin, 1996); *Tips for the Mathematics Teacher: Research-Based Strategies to Help Students Learn* (Corwin, 1998); *Advanced Euclidean Geometry: Excursions for Secondary Teachers and Students* (John Wiley, 2002); *Math Wonders: To Inspire Teachers and Students* (Association for Supervision and Curriculum Development, 2003); *Math Charmers: Tantalizing Tidbits for the Mind* (Prometheus Books, 2003); *Pi: A Biography of the World's Most Mysterious Number* (Prometheus Books, 2004); *Teaching Secondary School Mathematics: Techniques and Enrichment Units* (Merrill/Prentice Hall, 8th ed., 2009); *101+ Great Ideas to Introduce Key Concepts in Mathematics* (Corwin, 2006); *What Successful Math Teachers Do: Grades 6–12* (Corwin, 2006); *What Successful Math Teachers Do: Grades K–5* (Corwin, 2007); *Exemplary Practices for Math Teachers* (Association for Supervision and Curriculum Development, 2007); *The Fabulous Fibonacci Numbers* (Prometheus Books, 2007); *Problem-Solving Strategies for Efficient and Elegant Solutions: Grades 6–12* (Corwin, 2008); and *Mathematical Amazements and Surprises: Fascinating Figures and Noteworthy Numbers* (Prometheus Books, 2009).

 **Stephen Krulik** is Professor Emeritus of Mathematics Education at Temple University in Philadelphia. While at Temple University, Dr. Krulik was responsible for the undergraduate and graduate preparation of mathematics teachers for grades K–12, as well as the in-service alertness training of mathematics teachers at the graduate level. He teaches a wide variety of courses, among them the History of Mathematics, Methods of Teaching Mathematics, and The Teaching of Problem Solving. This latter course grew out of his interest in problem solving and reasoning in the mathematics classroom. His concern that students understand the beauty and value of problem solving as well as the ability to reason led to this book.

Dr. Krulik received his BA degree in mathematics from Brooklyn College of the City University of New York and his MA and EdD in mathematics education from Columbia University's Teachers College. Before coming to Temple University, he taught mathematics in the New York City public schools for 15 years. At Lafayette High School in Brooklyn, he created and implemented several courses designed to prepare students for the SAT examination, while stressing the art of problem solving as opposed to rote memorization of algorithms.

Nationally, Dr. Krulik has served as a member of the committee responsible for preparing the *Professional Standards for Teaching Mathematics* of the National Council of Teachers of Mathematics. He was also the editor of the NCTM's 1980 Yearbook *Problem Solving in School Mathematics.* Regionally, he served as president of the Association of Mathematics Teachers of New Jersey, was a member of the editorial team that produced the 1993 publication *The New Jersey Calculator Handbook,* and was the editor for their 1997 monograph *Tomorrow's Lessons.*

His major areas of interest are the teaching of problem solving and reasoning, materials for teaching mathematics, as well as comprehensive assessment in mathematics. He is the author and co-author of more than 30 books for teachers of mathematics, including the *Roads to Reasoning* (grades 1–8) and *Problem Driven Math* (grades 3–8). Dr. Krulik is also the problem-solving author for a major basal textbook series. Dr. Krulik is a frequent contributor to the professional journals in mathematics education. He has served as a consultant to, and has conducted many workshops for, school districts throughout the United States and Canada, as well as delivering major presentations in Vienna (Austria), Budapest (Hungary), Adelaide (Australia), Quebec (Canada) and San Juan (Puerto Rico). He is in great demand as a speaker at both national and international professional meetings, where his major focus is on preparing *all* students to reason and problem solve in their mathematics classroom, as well as in life.

1

An Introduction to Problem Solving

Problem solving has been an integral part of mathematics throughout recorded history. Over the past half century, there have been many vacillating agendas that have driven state curricula and ultimately the instruction of mathematics throughout the United States. Although many books have been written to address this all-important aspect of mathematics instruction over the past decades, the topic was not formally addressed until 1977, when the National Council of Supervisors of Mathematics (NCSM) pointed out that "learning to solve problems is the principal reason for studying mathematics" (NCSM 1977, 1). This marked the beginning of the problem-solving movement in school mathematics in the United States. More recently, the National Council of Teachers of Mathematics (NCTM), in their *Professional Standards for Teaching Mathematics*, stated that "Problem solving, reasoning and communication are processes that should pervade all mathematics instruction and should be modeled by teachers" (NCTM 1991, 95). Even earlier, in 1980, in its *Agenda for Action*, the NCTM stated that "Problem solving must be the focus of the curriculum" (NCTM 1980, 1). These comments are as valid today as they were then. In fact, what has changed is the approach to problem solving, not only as a separate topic of instruction, but also as a vehicle for teaching the skills and concepts of mathematics.

Today, problem solving is no longer merely another movement among the many that have appeared and disappeared in mathematics education. Rather, problem solving has now been accepted by most teachers as an integral part of their mathematics curriculum that must be taught alongside the arithmetic skills that are so necessary for success in school and in real life afterwards. In fact, problem solving provides the reason for teaching the skills of arithmetic.

Before we discuss problem solving, let's examine just what we mean by a "problem." A problem is a situation that confronts the learner, that requires resolution, and for which the path to the answer is not immediately known. It is this very definition of a problem that reduces many of the "word problems" teachers do from "problems" to mere "exercises." Teachers often group problems by types, and demonstrate to the class how to approach them. These might include problems dealing with uniform motion, age, mixture, percent, and so on. Usually, students are shown how to do one of these problems and told that the others are very similar and should be done the same way, albeit with different numbers! These we shall refer to as "exercises" rather than problems, because recognition of the type of problem immediately provides the learner with the path (or method) for arriving at the correct answer. Little thinking on the part of the students is required; rather, all they need do is recognize the type of problem and recall what the teacher's approach had been. Unfortunately, if the specific type of problem has not been taught, the children are often baffled, because they have not learned the new and different type of exercise. Although the problems in this book have been grouped by strategy for convenience, one should take note that once a strategy has been learned, it can then be applied to a variety of situations. Strategies are generic; they can be applied widely—exercise "types" cannot.

Now that we know what constitutes a problem, let's look at problem solving. Problem solving can be thought of in several different ways. First of all, problem solving may be considered a topic of instruction. That is, problem solving is a subject in the mathematics curriculum that must be taught to the children in the same way that multiplication, long division, percents, and so on, are taught. It can't be learned incidentally; it must be stressed and carefully taught! Second, problem solving may also be considered a mode of instruction. We can teach our mathematics classes using problem solving as the underlying thread to unite all the mathematics we teach. Problem solving provides a rationale for teaching the skills of arithmetic. Finally, problem solving is a way of thinking. That is, students cannot expect to learn to be problem solvers without careful structure of the process. Although some students intuitively may be good problem solvers, most of our students must be taught how to think, how to reason, and how to problem solve.

The way students approach problems will vary from child to child. However, one thing is clear. They will most often approach a problem based upon their backgrounds and experiences. This can range from recognizing a problem as similar to one previously seen in class, or to taking on homework exercises similar to those discussed in class that day. In most cases, the student is not doing any problem solving, any reasoning, or any thinking. The student is simply mimicking (or copying) the skills learned earlier in class. If they do not recognize the type of problem (exercise), they may just sit back and be baffled. Students must be given the appropriate background, instruction, and support if they are to become effective problem solvers. They must learn how to solve problems and practice this sometimes elusive skill.

It is our goal in this book to make teachers aware of the ways that different problem-solving strategies can be used to provide elegant and efficient solutions to problems. Sometimes, teachers unwittingly convey to their students that there is one and only one way to solve a problem. The teacher may discourage the students from trying different strategies to solve problems, or may insist upon a unique strategy when approaching a problem. If the children are to become problem solvers, then the classroom must be a nonthreatening environment. Students must be free to express themselves and to try what they think is the way they wish to solve the problem, even if the approach leads to a dead end. The answer is not as important as the solution process used to obtain that answer.

One fact that teachers comment on, over and over, is the lack of a single resource containing sufficient problems to enable them to teach the strategies of problem solving. In fact, some teachers at the upper elementary school level are not even aware of the strategies that exist. They may recognize a few strategies from the textbook they use in class, but they are not aware of the existence of some of the other strategies that will be discussed in this book. The book is designed for the upper elementary school teacher who has a sincere desire to help his or her students succeed as problem solvers. It is divided up into chapters, each devoted to a specific strategy widely used in problem solving. The strategies are presented and applied to many problems so that you can more easily present the strategies to your students. Select the problems that are appropriate for your students' age and mathematical maturity. Use them as vehicles to teach the strategies of problem solving in your mathematics class. They are an excellent supplement to the problems and strategies that you will find in your textbook.

PROBLEM SOLVING ON ASSESSMENT TESTS

Most states are now requiring students to solve problems on the state mathematics tests. In addition to testing the children's abilities to master the basic skills of arithmetic, the test makers are placing a great emphasis on problem solving. Open-ended problems that do not have a single definite answer challenge the children to adapt their own knowledge and experiences to help solve the problems. Rubrics are designed to accurately score the student responses and provide guidance to teachers to help students become better reasoners, thinkers, and problem solvers. The students are confronted with problems that require careful thought and reasoning, but also a knowledge of the strategies to be used to solve the problems. There is, additionally, a heavy emphasis on having the students write a careful explanation of what they did and why they did it.

THE HEURISTICS OF PROBLEM SOLVING

In 1945, George Polya published a book titled *How to Solve It*. This book was the forerunner of the problem-solving movement long before it actually started. In this book, Polya discussed the use of "heuristics" as a plan for solving problems. Heuristics is the process by which a problem solver attempts various approaches to find the solution to a problem. His heuristic model contained four steps. The student must first *read* the problem and think about it. He or she must carefully identify what information is given and what is to be found. Excess information is eliminated. Next, the student decides upon a *plan*. A strategy is suggested to be used to solve the problem. In the third stage, the student applies the strategy that was selected and tries to solve the problem, so as to arrive at the correct answer. In the fourth and final step, the student *looks back* at his or her solution and answer to make certain that his or her work is correct and that the question asked has, indeed, been answered correctly. It is this four-step plan that is the basis for the heuristic plans in most textbooks today, regardless of the names given to the steps or even the number of steps suggested.

Notice that a heuristic plan is quite different from an algorithm. If a student recognizes the appropriate algorithm and applies it correctly, he or she is guaranteed to arrive at the correct answer. Because a heuristic plan is only a model or guide, it can be applied correctly without guaranteeing the correct answer. However, the heuristic model does provide a guide for solving problems in general.

HOW TO USE THIS BOOK

This book has been designed as a resource for the teacher of the upper elementary school grades (3–6). Problem solving should play a major role in all mathematics instruction. When we teach children to be problem solvers, we are teaching them to think and to reason, skills that will be critical for their entire lives—even beyond mathematics! And, if we are to succeed in teaching them to think, they need something about which to think. Problems provide this "something." We know that some teachers in the elementary school do not have an adequate source of problems to illustrate each of the problem-solving strategies. In most cases, you are limited to the problems that are provided in the class textbook. If students do not learn a particular strategy on the first or second attempt, the opportunity to reteach the strategy may not occur again in the book. We hope this book will remedy this dilemma.

Begin by reading through this book. Each chapter begins with a problem—posed for the teacher—that is representative of the particular strategy to be discussed. Take your time working out the problem, and then compare your solution with that suggested. Take some time to work out several of the problems intended for the students. Then compare your solutions with those suggested. Read the section titled *Teaching Notes*. When you feel comfortable, use these problems to teach this strategy to your students. Teachers typically learn a subject thoroughly when they teach it! Be ready to accept any suggestions made by the children. Carry out their suggestions to see if they provide an alternate solution to the problem, or merely lead to a dead end. In either case, valuable mathematics will be learned by the children. Notice that we refer to "answer" and "solution" as different. The *solution* is the entire process from the original encounter with the problem to the very end. The *answer* is the end product of the solution. As we have stated before, the answer must be correct, but we must put more importance on the process that was used to arrive at the answer.

PROBLEM DECKS

You should begin to create a math-problem set of cards (say, 5" × 9"). Every time you encounter a math problem that is appropriate for your students, write it on a card together with its solution and answer. On the back of the card, you might put the strategy or strategies used to solve the problem, together with the mathematics topic needed to solve the problem, or where it might fit in your curriculum. Feel free to copy problems directly from this book; they will provide an excellent starter set of problems. Keep adding to your set of cards whenever you encounter a problem you feel is appropriate for your students.

Some teachers may prefer to develop their problem deck on their computer. That is, they set up a series of folders of strategies, and each time place the problem where it is most appropriate. Provide the same information on this electronic math-problem set as you would on the cards. In any case, whenever you need a problem, take it from your deck and use it with the students.

THE STRATEGIES OF PROBLEM SOLVING

We have divided the rest of the book into nine strategies. Each chapter is devoted to an individual strategy, with many problems designed to illustrate how the strategy is applied. Here is the list of strategies:

- Organizing the Data
  - Creating a List
  - Making a Table
- Intelligent Guessing and Testing
- Solving a Simpler, Equivalent Problem
- Acting It Out/Simulating the Action
- Working Backwards
- Finding a Pattern
- Logical Reasoning
- Making a Drawing
- Adopting a Different Point of View

Your own textbook may have some or all of these strategies included. Not all of the strategies are appropriate for every grade or even for every student within a given grade. You must decide what is appropriate for your students and act accordingly. You might decide to modify a particular problem by making the numbers simpler or asking for only part of the problem. This is up to you—no one knows your students better than you do!

2

Organizing Data

Organizing data is an important step in analyzing any set of data. Sometimes, the data is numerical (as we would expect), and other times, it might be of a more visual nature. For example, consider the problem of determining the shortest route to take from a given point to a destination. The way in which we list the routes—organizing them by order of proximity—can be a significant factor in selecting the best route. In mathematics, some problems present an excessive amount of data. How this data gets organized can often determine whether or not the problem can be solved. A table is one way to organize the data in a problem. In many problems involving the guess-and-test strategy, for example, a table provides an excellent way of keeping track of the data and determining whether the next guess should be a larger or smaller one. An organized list is often used instead of a table, and may be a bit less formal. Both the list and the table perform the same function—that is, they are used to keep track of data in the problem and lead the way to its solution. In some problems, the list itself may be the answer to the question that was asked.

APPLYING THE ORGANIZING DATA STRATEGY

Consider the following problem:

> David and Lisa are in a charity tennis tournament at the local tennis club. The first player to win either two consecutive games or a total

of three games wins the match. In how many different ways can their match be played?

We can begin to resolve this problem by writing out all the possible scenarios. That is, suppose Lisa wins the first game, loses the second, wins the third, and wins the fourth. Alternatively, David might win the first game, lose the second, win the third, win the fourth, and so on. Obviously, there are too many ways to ensure that we'll have them all.

At first, there seem to be too many different ways to count. However, let's organize the data in a careful manner by making an exhaustive list of the possibilities. The first half of the list contains all winning situations when Lisa wins the first game. The second half of the list contains all the winning situations when David wins the first game.

Lisa—1st game	David—1st game
LL	DD
LDD	DLL
LDLL	DLDD
LDLDL	DLDLD
LDLDD	DLDLL

Thus, there are ten possible ways the match can be played.

CHAPTER TEACHING NOTES

Students do not necessarily arrive in your classroom possessing an ability to effectively organize data so as to solve problems. Such students—the large majority—initially may be confused and bewildered when faced with many of the problems we have posed in this chapter. Not knowing where or how to start, they may decide to guess randomly. Rather than systematically recording relevant data in an appropriate list or table, they may simulate independent and disconnected solutions with blocks, coins, or other manipulatives. Unfortunately, although such simulation might eventually result in a complete solution, its very lack of systematic thinking provides little assurance. The ability to organize data for problem solving is something you need to teach and your students need to practice and learn. These problems should provide relevant exercise. Nonetheless, there is substantial teaching involved. Without going into details—this is, after all, a book on problem solving—we note that students need to know how to create tables: what categories to record and how many, for example, trial solutions. Students need to know how to read tables: how to identify and interpret patterns and relationships; how to pick out the correct answer; and, keeping in mind the nature of problem solving, whether organizing data is an appropriate solution technique.

These are not things to be taught independently of the problems in this chapter, but are to be taught in conjunction. These practices can be modeled, discussed, and critiqued, and each of these problems modeled and discussed. Students need to understand and appreciate the power and elegance such strategies provide when data is thoughtfully and systematically organized and interpreted.

PROBLEMS FOR STUDENTS

Problem 2.1 (Grades 4–6)

Jean has 55 blocks to stack in a triangle display in the store window. She would like the top of the triangular display to have one block, the one below it to have two blocks, the one below that to have three blocks, and so on. Is it possible to make such a triangle with all 55 blocks, and if so, how many rows will the triangle have?

Solution: Let's begin at the top of our triangle with one block and continue along until all 55 blocks are used. This can be best done by setting up a table to record the progress of this reverse building.

Row Number	Number of Blocks in Row	Total Number of Blocks Used
1	1	1
2	2	3
3	3	6
4	4	10
5	5	15
6	6	21
7	7	28
8	8	36
9	9	45
10	10	55

From the table, we can see that after 10 rows, we used 55 blocks.

Answer: It can be done, and it would require 10 rows to use exactly 55 blocks.

Problem 2.2 (Grades 5–7)

December 12 and December 24 are interesting dates because they are multiples of 12, and December is the 12th month of the year. How many days in a non-leap year are multiples of their month-number?

Solution: To find the dates that are multiples of their month-number we can make an organized list to have a better overview of the pattern. In order to solve this problem, we need to list the month and its number and then the dates that are the multiples of that number.

Month	Month #	Multiples	Number of Multiples
January	1	all	31
February	2	even dates	14
March	3	3, 6, 9, 12, 15, 18, 21, 24, 27, 30	10
April	4	4, 8, 12, 16, 20, 24, 28	7
May	5	5, 10, 15, 20, 25, 30	6
June	6	6, 12, 18, 24, 30	5
July	7	7, 14, 21, 28	4
August	8	8, 16, 24	3
September	9	9, 18, 27	3
October	10	10, 20, 30	3
November	11	11, 22	2
December	12	12, 24	2

We can add the number of multiples to find our answer. This problem might serve well to lead to a discussion on multiples and factors.

Answer: There are 90 days that are multiples of their month-number.

Problem 2.3 (Grades 5–7)

Tomorrow is the first day of school, and Lana is choosing her outfit to wear. She has black and green slacks; 3 blouses (red, flowers, plaid); and 2 sweaters (beige and cream). How many different outfits can she make consisting of one pair of slacks, one blouse, and one sweater?

Solution: There are a lot of possibilities. Let's list the outfits she might choose. Be certain to make the list organized so we can be sure we have all the possibilities.

Slacks	Blouse	Sweater
Black	Red	Beige
Black	Red	Cream
Black	Flowers	Beige
Black	Flowers	Cream
Black	Plaid	Beige
Black	Plaid	Cream
Green	Red	Beige
Green	Red	Cream
Green	Flowers	Beige
Green	Flowers	Cream
Green	Plaid	Beige
Green	Plaid	Cream

The organized list includes all the possible outfits she might select and suggests another solution from which some students might benefit. They can see from the list that for the black slacks there are three possible blouses, and for each blouse there are two possible sweaters. This means there are $3 \times 2 = 6$ possible combinations for the black slacks. Because there are two types of slacks (black and green), we double the number of combinations to get 12.

Answer: She has 12 outfits from which to choose.

Problem 2.4 (Grades 5–7)

The lunch menu for Monday is Mexican. They will serve three kinds of burritos: chicken, beef, or vegetarian. You can choose either a flour or a corn tortilla. You can also decide whether to have hot sauce or not. How many different combinations are there from which to choose?

Solution: This problem is similar to the previous one. Let's make an organized list to be certain we include all the possibilities. Start with the filling, then the tortilla, and finally sauce or not.

Filling	Tortilla	Sauce
Beef	Corn	Yes
Beef	Corn	No
Beef	Flour	Yes
Beef	Flour	No
Chicken	Corn	Yes
Chicken	Corn	No
Chicken	Flour	Yes
Chicken	Flour	No
Vegetarian	Corn	Yes
Vegetarian	Corn	No
Vegetarian	Flour	Yes
Vegetarian	Flour	No

These are all the possible combinations we can make. Notice how the list is organized to ensure all combinations.

Answer: There are 12 different combinations from which to select.

Problem 2.5 (Grades 3–5)

You have a lot of dimes, nickels, and pennies in your pocket. You reach in and pull out three of the coins without looking. What are the different amounts of money you could have taken from your pocket?

Solution: Let's make an organized list. Be sure to include all possible combinations of coins. One solution is to start with the maximum number of dimes, and then reduce the number of dimes by 1 after all possible combinations for that number of dimes have been listed.

Dimes	Nickels	Pennies	
3	0	0	= 30¢
2	1	0	= 25¢
2	0	1	= 21¢
1	2	0	= 20¢
1	1	1	= 16¢
1	0	2	= 12¢
0	3	0	= 15¢
0	2	1	= 11¢
0	1	2	= 7¢
0	0	3	= 3¢

Check to make sure all the amounts are different. In this problem, the list is the actual answer.

Answer: There are 10 different sums you could make with three coins. The answers are 30¢, 25¢, 21¢, 20¢, 16¢, 12¢, 15¢, 11¢, 7¢, and 3¢.

Problem 2.6 (Grades 3–5)

Harlow, Indira, Jessica, and Karl are taking karate lessons. They will work out in pairs. How many different pairs are possible?

Solution: Let's make a list of the possible pairs. We organize the list by considering all possible pairs beginning with Harlow.

Harlow—Indira

Harlow—Jessica

Harlow—Karl

Now we consider all the pairs beginning with Indira. Notice, however, that Indira—Harlow is a repeat of Harlow—Indira, already counted.

Indira—Jessica

Indira—Karl

Finally, consider pairs beginning with Jessica that have not already been counted.

Jessica—Karl

Answer: There are 6 possible pairs of students.

Problem 2.7 (Grades 4–6)

At the grand opening of the new T-Shirt Cottage store, they are offering prizes to the first 96 people in line. At 7:00 a.m., there were 3 people in line. At 7:15, 3 more people got in line, for a total of 6 people. At 7:30, 6 more people arrived, so there were 12 people in line. Every 15 minutes, the same number of people who are already in line arrive. At what time will the 96th person be in line?

Solution: We can make a table to show what is happening during each 15-minute interval. Keep going until we find the time the 96th person arrives.

Time	Number Arriving	Number in Line
7:00	3	3
7:15	3	6
7:30	6	12
7:45	12	24
8:00	24	48
8:15	**48**	**96**

Answer: There will be 96 people in line at 8:15.

Problem 2.8 (Grades 4–6)

In the school store, pencils cost 15¢ each and erasers cost 10¢ each. There is no tax. Max wants to spend exactly $2.00 on pencils and erasers. How many of each can she buy?

Solution: Let's make a table. We'll include a column for the number of each kind of item as well as the cost. The total cost must always be $2.00.

Erasers		Pencils		
Number	Cost	Number	Cost	Total Cost
20	**$2.00**	**0**	**0**	**$2.00**
19	$1.90	0	0	$1.90
18	$1.80	1	.15	$1.95
17	**$1.70**	**2**	**.30**	**$2.00**
16	$1.60	2	.30	$1.90
15	$1.50	3	.45	$1.95
14	**$1.40**	**4**	**.60**	**$2.00**
13	$1.30	4	.60	$1.90
12	$1.20	5	.75	$1.95
11	**$1.10**	**6**	**.90**	**$2.00**
10	$1.00	6	.90	$1.90
9	$.90	7	$1.05	$1.95
8	**$.80**	**8**	**$1.20**	**$2.00**
7	$.70	8	$1.20	$1.90
6	$.60	9	$1.35	$1.95
5	**$.50**	**10**	**$1.50**	**$2.00**
4	$.40	10	$1.50	$1.90
3	$.30	11	$1.65	$1.95
2	**$.20**	**12**	**$1.80**	**$2.00**
1	$.10	12	$1.80	$1.90
0	0	13	$1.95	$1.95

Answer: There are 7 possibilities for Max to spend exactly $2.00 on pencils and erasers. They are 20 erasers and 0 pencils, 17 erasers and 2 pencils, 14 erasers and 4 pencils, 11 erasers and 6 pencils, 8 erasers and 8 pencils, 5 erasers and 10 pencils, and 2 erasers and 12 pencils.

Teaching Notes: Discuss with the class the many patterns that appear in the table. Also emphasize that a problem may have more than one correct answer.

Problem 2.9 (Grades 4–5)

Alice and Benjamin are brother and sister. Alice is 3 and Benjamin is 12. How old will they each be when Benjamin is 2½ times as old as Alice?

Solution: Let's make a table to show their respective ages each year.

Alice	3	4	5	**6**	7	8
Benjamin	12	13	14	**15**	16	17

The table shows their ages each year. We can find the ages when Benjamin is exactly 2½ times as old as Alice.

Answer: Benjamin will be 15 and Alice 6 when he is 2½ times as old as she is.

Problem 2.10 (Grades 5–7)

A family goes to the movies. Adult tickets cost $6.00 each and children's tickets cost $4.00 each. The family spent $26.00. How many adults and how many children went to the movies?

Solution: Let's make a table showing all the various possibilities for adult tickets and children's tickets and find the one that gives $26.00.

Adults @ $6.00	Children @ $4.00	Total Cost
1 = $6.00	1 = $4.00	$10.00
1 = $6.00	2 = $8.00	$14.00
1 = $6.00	3 = $12.00	$18.00
1 = $6.00	4 = $16.00	$22.00
1 = $6.00	**5 = $20.00**	**$26.00***
2 = $12.00	1 = $4.00	$16.00
2 = $12.00	2 = $8.00	$20.00
2 = $12.00	3 = $12.00	$24.00
2 = $12.00	4 = $16.00	$28.00
3 = $18.00	1 = $4.00	$22.00
3 = $18.00	**2 = $8.00**	**$26.00***
4 = $24.00	1 = $4.00	$28.00

Answer: There are 2 possible answers: 1 adult and 5 children or 3 adults and 2 children.

Problem 2.11 (Grades 3–4)

There is a monorail running around the amusement park. The monorail car has no passengers when it leaves the terminal. At the first stop, it picks up 5 people. At the second stop, 4 people get on and 2 people get off. At the third stop, 5 people get on and no one gets off. At the fourth stop, 1 person gets on and 4 people get off. How many passengers are now on the monorail car?

Solution: Let's make a chart to simulate the events.

Stop #	People On	People Off	Number on the Monorail
Terminal	0	0	0
#1	5	0	5
#2	4	2	7
#3	5	0	12
#4	1	4	9

We can also organize the data by adding all the total number of people getting on the monorail, and then the total of all the people getting off the monorail. This will yield the answer quite quickly:

On Monorail = $5 + 4 + 5 + 1 = 15$

Off Monorail = $2 + 4 = 6$

Remaining on Monorail = $15 - 6 = 9$

Answer: There are 9 people left on the monorail at the end of the trip.

Problem 2.12 (Grades 3–4)

At the bottom of the pile of junk in the lake were a cup, a jar, a shoe, and an old tire. A fish, a frog, a crab, and a snake came along. The snake went into the jar and fell asleep. The crab crawled into the shoe. The fish won't go near the tire. Into which object did each creature go?

Solution: To organize the data in a manageable manner, make a matrix and fill in the clues. Remember, a "Yes" in a column means an "X" in all other items in that column and row. Thus, the first clue tells us that the snake went into the jar. This means a "Yes" in that cell of the matrix. It also means no one else could be in the jar (all Xs in that column) nor could the snake be anywhere else (all Xs in that row). Continue in a similar manner using the clues, one at a time.

	Cup	Jar	Shoe	Tire
Fish	Yes	X	X	X
Frog	X	X	X	Yes
Crab	X	X	Yes	X
Snake	X	Yes	X	X

The matrix shows which creature was in each object.

Answer: The fish is in the cup, the frog is in the tire, the crab is in the shoe, and the snake is in the jar.

You might be interested to note that this problem reappears in Chapter 8 as Problem 8.6 because it is appropriate there as well.

Problem 2.13 (Grades 3–4)

The school music club is going to a concert. There will be only 2 teachers for every 9 students. There are 16 teachers on the trip. How many students will there be?

Solution: One approach to solving this problem is to use chips of two different colors. Suppose the teachers are represented by red chips and the students by yellow ones. We can then actually show 9 yellow chips for every 2 red chips. We can set up a total of 8 groups until we have 16 red chips and count the number of yellow chips. This will yield the answer.

A more elegant solution is to make a table and follow it out to the 16 teachers:

Teachers	2	4	6	8	10	12	14	**16**
Students	9	18	27	36	45	54	63	**72**

This is actually a problem in ratio and proportion. A more mathematically sophisticated solution is to set up the proportion $\frac{2}{9} = \frac{16}{x}$. If we solve for x, we obtain 72. Of course, this approach is beyond the experiences of most students in grades 3–4.

Answer: There will be 72 students going to the concert.

Problem 2.14 (Grades 6–7)

There are 6 points, no three of which lie on the same line. How many straight line segments are needed to connect every possible pair of dots?

Solution: By organizing data, we take the six points and begin by connecting point *A* to each of the other points. Then we have 5 line segments, *AB, AC, AD, AE,* and *AF* (see Figure 2.1).

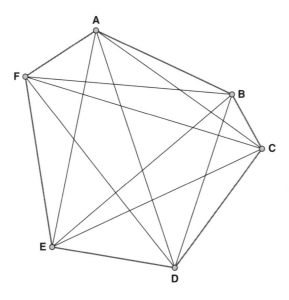

Figure 2.1

Now consider point *B*. In similar fashion, we have *BA, BC, BD, BE,* and *BF*. But *BA* is the same line segment as *AB,* so it need not be drawn again. Thus, from point *B,* we have only 4 segments. If we continue this pattern, we have 3 segments from point *C* (*CD, CE,* and *CF,* while *AC* and *BC* have been drawn). Thus we have $5 + 4 + 3 + 2 + 1 = 15$ lines drawn.

Answer: There will be 15 line segments to connect the points as required.

Problem 2.15 (Grades 4–6)

A hot dog vendor buys her hot dogs in packages of 36. She buys the hot-dog buns in packages of 20. What is the smallest number of hot dogs and hot dog buns she must buy to have an equal amount of hot dogs and buns with none left over?

Solution: Let's make a table and organize our data. When she buys 180 rolls and 180 hot dogs, she can do it with packages and have none left over.

No. of Pkgs	1	2	3	4	5	6	7	8	9
Hot Dogs	36	72	108	144	**180**				
Buns	20	40	60	80	100	120	140	160	**180**

Answer: She must buy 180 hot dogs (5 packages) and 180 buns (9 packages).

Teaching Notes: This problem is an example of finding the lowest common multiple of two numbers. It provides an excellent opportunity for you to discuss this concept with the children.

Problem 2.16 (Grades 4–6)

The new jeans store at 64 Fifth Avenue is giving prizes to the first 64 people who are in line when they open at 9:30 a.m. At 8:05, there were 8 people in line. At 8:10, there were 16 people in line. At 8:15, there were 24 people in line. If this pattern continues, at what time will there be 64 people in line?

Solution: Children often act out this type of problem. They can use other students, or chips to represent the people. A more efficient solution, however, is to organize the data in a table.

Time	8:05	8:10	8:15	8:20	8:25	8:30	8:35	**8:40**	8:45	8:50
Arrive	8	8	8	8	8	8	8	8		
In line	8	16	24	32	40	48	56	**64**		

Answer: At 8:40, there will be 64 people in line.

Teaching Notes: You may have to help the children recognize the patterns in the problem; that is, 8 people arrive every 5 minutes.

Problem 2.17 (Grades 5–7)

Michelle bought a used bicycle for $45. She fixed it up and then sold it for $60. A few weeks later, she bought it back for $75 and then sold it a month later for $95. Did Michelle make money, lose money or break even? If she made or lost money, how much did she make or lose?

Solution: An elegant approach to solve this is to organize your data in parts. Let's examine each pair of transactions in order:

> She bought the bicycle for $45 and sold it for $60. Profit of $15.
> She bought the bicycle for $75 and sold it for $95. Profit of $20.

Answer: Michelle made a total profit of $15 + $20 = $35.

Teaching Notes: You may recognize this as a variation on an often-quoted problem. Nevertheless, it is a good problem to use with your class. The fact that she paid more for the bike when she bought it back is irrelevant. Each time she bought and sold the bicycle, she made a profit. Some students might wish to add her costs ($45 + $75 = $120) and her total profits ($60 + $95 = $155). She made a total profit of $155 − $120 = $35.

3

Intelligent Guessing and Testing

We use an "intelligent guessing and testing" strategy in our everyday life experiences and are often not even aware that we are using it. For example, if you are mixing paints to match a given color, you tend to try and test till you get the desired result. Although this strategy does not sound very mathematical, it is a frequently used strategy. Some books refer to it as "trial and error." But it is *more* than that! This strategy is extremely powerful and quite sophisticated. The student makes a guess (and it must be an *intelligent* guess, not just an uninformed stab at the problem) and then proceeds to test that guess within the conditions of the problem. If the guess isn't correct, the student makes another guess. Each guess that follows is based upon the results obtained from the previous guesses. If the result of the testing was too small, the next guess should be a little bit larger; if the result was too large, the next guess should be smaller. Usually, a table or a list is used to organize the information from each successive guess and the results of that guess. The process continues until the child arrives at a guess that solves the problem.

APPLYING THE INTELLIGENT GUESSING AND TESTING STRATEGY

Consider the following problem:

Barbara took a 20-question multiple-choice test. The test was scored +5 for each correct answer, –2 for each wrong answer, and 0 if the question was omitted. Barbara scored a 44, even though she omitted some questions. How many questions did Barbara omit?

You might attempt to solve this algebraically. That is, let

x = the number of questions answered correctly
y = the number of questions answered incorrectly
z = the number of questions omitted.

Then, writing out the conditions of the problem would give

$$x + y + z = 20$$
$$5x - 2y + 0z = 44.$$

Effectively, you now have only two equations containing three variables.

Such a system of equations could be solved rather nicely by the strategy of Diophantine analysis. However, it also has a straightforward solution using intelligent guessing and testing. Examine the number of questions Barbara had correct. It must be at least 10, because if she had answered only 9 correctly, she would have received a score of $9 \times 5 = 45$, and by subtracting an even number, she could never end up with 44.

Correct (+5)	Wrong (–2)	Omitted (0)	Score (44)	# of Questions (20)
8	Impossible		$40 - 2 \times$ (# wrong)	
9	Impossible	0	$45 - 2 \times$ (# wrong)	
10	3	7	44	20
11	Impossible			
12	8	0	44	20
13	Impossible			
14	13	0	44	21

With 10 correct, Barbara would have had 3 wrong for a score of 44. Thus, she would have omitted 7 questions. This is a correct answer, but is it the only answer? Suppose Barbara had answered 11 questions correctly. There is no way she could arrive at 44 by subtracting an even number from 55. Therefore, 11 is impossible. Suppose we guess 12 correct. Then, $12 \times 5 = 60$ and $60 - 16 = 44$, which means she had 12 correct, 8 wrong, and none omitted. However, this contradicts the statement of the original problem. If Barbara answers 13 questions correctly, there is, as with 11 answered correctly, no way she could arrive at 44 for a score. If she answers 14 questions correctly, she could arrive at a score of 44 with 13 incorrect answers; however, there were only 20 questions on the test. By continuing this pattern, we see that for 16 and 18 questions answered correctly, there is no possible solution. Thus, the score of "omitted 7" is the only possible solution. By guessing and testing, we arrived at the answer in an efficient manner and have confidence that our answer is unique.

CHAPTER TEACHING NOTES

As we have emphasized, central to using this strategy is that a student make a series of systematic, informed, and validated guesses. The process begins with an informed guess. This step is crucial and rests heavily on the prior mathematics knowledge a student brings and how the problem has been contextualized. In the problem above, for example, we need to understand that a negative number of points results in subtraction and that the score for a certain number of right or wrong answers is obtained through multiplication. Although all of this may seem obvious to you, students are not necessarily comfortable with such ideas and, as the consequence of their misunderstandings, may make ineffectual and somewhat random conjectures. Much of the resulting confusion and frustration can be addressed by briefly discussing the meaning of a particular problem with the whole class prior to students beginning independent or group work. With younger students, you may wish to agree on an initial guess as a whole class.

The next step is no less crucial. Interesting mathematics problems, as we hope these are, are those in which the solution is not immediately obvious. Thus, an informed initial guess often is not among the answers. In this case, a student will need to revise his or her guess in some intelligent fashion. For example, if one guesses that the solution to the equation

$$25 + x = 35$$

is 5, testing shows that $25 + 5 = 30$. Hence, a better guess might be 6, giving the sum of 31. Subsequent guesses might be 8 and 11, giving sums of 33 and 36, respectively. If we have recorded these guesses and their consequences, we can see that an answer likely lies between 8 and 11. Hence, together with a revised guess is the need for a systematic approach. Students need to be encouraged, as we have previously noted, to keep their guesses and the consequences of those guesses in some organized fashion. Such records will be invaluable for subsequent *informed* guessing.

PROBLEMS FOR STUDENTS

Problem 3.1 (Grades 4–6)

A man was making out his will. He had $1600 to divide among his three sons. The oldest was to get $200 more than the middle son. The middle son was to get $100 more than the youngest son. How much did each son get?

Solution: We can use the guess and test strategy. Let's make a table to keep track of our guesses as we test each guess.

Guess #	Youngest	Middle	Oldest	Total
1	$100	$200	$400	$700 (Too small)
2	$200	$300	$500	$1000 (Too small)
3	$300	$400	$600	$1300 (Still too small)
4	$400	$500	$700	$1600 (Yes!)

We have the answer from the table.

Answer: The youngest son gets $400, the middle son gets $500, and the oldest son gets $700.

Problem 3.2 (Grades 3–5)

A baby alligator had a body plus tail length that was exactly 4 times as large as his head. From the tip of his nose to the tip of his tail, the alligator is exactly 35 inches long. How long is its head?

Solution: Let's make a series of guesses about the head, body and tail, and total length. We'll make a table and keep track of the guesses as we test each guess.

Guess #	Head	Body & Tail	Total Length
1	3"	12"	15" (Too small)
2	8"	32"	40" (Too large)
3	5"	20"	25" (Too small)
4	7"	28"	35" (Yes!)

Some students might recognize that, because the head is 1 part and the body is 4 times as large, we have a total of 5 equal parts. Thus, $35 \div 5 = 7$, the size of the head.

Answer: The alligator's head is 7" long.

Problem 3.3 (Grades 3–5)

Ian and Amanda were counting the number of comic books in their collections. Ian said to Amanda, "Give me one of your comics and we'll have the same number." Amanda thought for a moment and then replied, "Give me one of your comics and I'll have exactly twice as many as you do." How many comics did each of them have?

Solution: Some logic can be applied to the problem to make our guesses easier. It is apparent from the difference 1 comic book makes that the numbers must be rather small. Furthermore, if Ian's giving one away makes them equal, they must be two apart . . .

Now we can use the guess and test strategy. Let's make our first guess at 3 and 5. Now, if Amanda gives Ian 1 comic book, they will each have 4. But if Ian gives Amanda one of his comic books, she will have 6 and he will have 2. That is three times as many. No good. Let's try another guess, say, 4 and 6. If Amanda gives Ian one of her books, they will each have 5. But if he gives Amanda one of his, she will have 7 and he will have 3. Close, but not quite right. Let's try 5 and 7. If Amanda gives Ian one of her comic books, they will each have 6. If Ian gives Amanda one of his, she will have 8 and he will have 4, exactly twice as many. That's right! Amanda has 7 comic books and Ian has 5.

Answer: Ian must have 5 comic books and Amanda must have 7.

Problem 3.4 (Grades 4–6)

The Salad Works just opened its new store in the mall. The very first day they sold 4 dozen or more but fewer than 5 dozen salads. They sold twice as many pasta salads as they did chicken salads. They sold $\frac{1}{3}$ as many chicken salads as they did tuna salads. How many of each could they have sold?

Solution: The problem contains a great deal of data. Make a table to organize the facts so that we can see what's taking place in the problem. Let's use the guess and test strategy. Our first guess might be that they sold 6 chicken salads.

Chicken	Tuna	Pasta	Total	
6	18	12	36	Too small
7	21	14	42	Too small
8	24	16	48	Possible
9	27	18	54	Possible
10	30	20	60	Too large

Answer: There is more than one possible answer to this problem:

They sold 8 chicken salads, 24 tuna salads, 16 pasta salads

or

They sold 9 chicken salads, 27 tuna salads, 18 pasta salads.

These are the only possibilities *between* 4 dozen (48) and 5 dozen (60).

Teaching Notes: Rarely do students see problems in the math classroom with more than one correct answer. It is a good idea to discuss this situation with the class.

Problem 3.5 (Grade 4–6)

Mary baked 37 muffins for her party. She put the blueberry muffins into bags of 5 and the corn muffins into bags of 3. How many of each kind of muffin did she bake?

Solution: We will use the guess and test strategy. We'll organize our guesses with a table. Put the blueberry muffins in groups of 5 and see how many are left over from 37.

Blueberry	Total Number	Corn	
5	37	32	(No. 32 is not divisible by 3)
10	**37**	**27**	**(Yes. 27 is divisible by 3)**
15	37	22	(No. 22 is not divisible by 3)
20	37	17	(No. 17 is not divisible by 3)
25	**37**	**12**	**(Yes. 12 is divisible by 3)**
30	37	7	(No. 7 is not divisible by 3)
35	37	2	(No. 2 is not divisible by 3)

Our table shows that there aren't any other possibilities where the sum is 37.

Answer: There are two answers possible. She baked 10 blueberry muffins and 27 corn muffins or she baked 25 blueberry muffins and 12 corn muffins.

Problem 3.6 (Grades 3–4)

The following is the menu in the school cafeteria:

Apple 25¢	Chocolate Milk 30¢	Grilled Cheese Sandwich 75¢
Granola Bar 45¢	Orange Juice 35¢	Veggie Burger $1.10
Ice Cream 50¢	Milk 25¢	Slice of Pizza 85¢

Liu spent $1.30 and bought exactly 2 items. What did he buy for lunch?

Solution: We use the guess and test strategy:

Let's guess milk and veggie burger. That's 25¢ + $1.10 = $1.35. Too large.

Let's guess grilled cheese and ice cream. That's 75¢ + 30¢ = $1.05. Too small.

Let's guess veggie burger and granola bar. That's $1.10 + 45¢ = $1.55. Too large.

Let's guess pizza and granola. That's 85¢ + 45¢ = $1.30. That works!

Answer: He bought a slice of pizza and a granola bar.

Problem 3.7 (Grades 3–5)

There are 2 baby pandas at the local zoo. They are named Tristan and Isolde. The people are voting to see which one is their favorite. Exactly 105 people voted. Tristan was favored by 2½ times as many people as Isolde. How many votes did each panda receive?

Solution: We'll use the guess and test strategy. A table will help us keep track of our guesses. Let's start with 50 votes for Isolde and compute 2½ times as many for Tristan.

Isolde	Tristan	Total Votes
50	125	175 (Too many votes)
40	100	140 (Still too many)
30	75	105 (Yes!)

We have the answer. The total is 105 and 75 is exactly 2½ times as many as 30.

Answer: Isolde received 30 votes; Tristan received 75 votes.

Problem 3.8 (Grades 5–7)

The local football team won their last game of the season by a score of 17 to 0. Even though they did not score a safety (2 points), they did manage to score more points in each quarter than they had scored in the previous quarter. How many points did they score in each quarter?

   The problem requires a knowledge of the scoring during a football game. The possible scores are 3 points for a field goal, 6 points for a touchdown, 7 points for a touchdown followed by an extra point kick, and 8 points for a touchdown followed by a 2-point conversion.

Solution: Using the guess and test strategy, we start with 0 points in the first quarter and proceed from there. The only possible way to score 17 points without a safety and a higher number in each quarter is 0, 3, 6, and 8. Thus, they scored 0 points in the first quarter, 3 points in the second quarter, 6 points in the third quarter, and 8 points in the fourth quarter. Notice that the 6 points could either be 2 field goals or 1 touchdown (with a missed extra-point kick).

Answer: They scored 0, 3, 6, and 8 in the four quarters, respectively.

Problem 3.9 (Grades 3–4)

Whenever I put a nickel in my piggy bank, my dad puts in 3 dimes. I opened the bank and found we had exactly 60 coins. How much money is in the piggy bank?

Solution: The guess and test strategy with a table to keep track of the guesses provides an efficient solution.

# Nickels	Value	# Dimes	Value	# Coins	Value
5	$0.25	15	$1.50	20	$1.75 (Too small)
10	$0.50	30	$3.00	40	$3.50 (Better)
15	$0.75	45	$4.50	60	$5.25 (Yes!)

   This problem could also have used the logical reasoning method. If each time there were four coins added to the sum (that is, 1 nickel and three dimes), and there were 60 coins in the bank, then this event of putting four coins in the bank had to have occurred $60 \div 4 = 15$ times. That means there were 15 nickels ($0.75) and 45 dimes ($4.50) for a total of $5.25 in the bank.

Answer: The 60 coins have a value of $5.25.

Problem 3.10 (Grades 5–7)

The tickets for the school Olympics went on sale Monday morning at 10:00 a.m. Tickets were priced at $10 and $17. By 3:00 p.m., they had sold 330 tickets and the total sales were $4,910. How many of each kind of ticket were sold that day?

Solution: There are only a finite number of possibilities, so we can try to use the guess and test strategy. Let's make a table to keep track of our guesses and tests. We can begin by assuming that one-half of the tickets were sold at each price. It is wise to let individual students narrow in on the right answer in their own way—that is, without guiding them. This will be a fruitful exercise for them.

Number of $10 Tickets	Amount	Number of $17 Tickets	Amount	Total Amount
165	$1,650	165	$2,805	$4,455 (Too small)
145	$1,450	185	$3,145	$4,595 (Better—still too small)
125	$1,250	205	$3,485	$4,735 (Still too small)
105	$1,050	225	$3,825	$4,875 (Getting very close)
100	$1,000	230	$3,910	$4,910 (Yes!)

Answer: They sold 100 tickets at $10 each and 230 tickets at $17 each.

Teaching Notes: Some students may worry about the 10:00 a.m. and 3:00 p.m. given in the problem, as they may have been taught that every number in a problem should be used. This is an excellent opportunity for you to discuss the idea of data that is irrelevant to a problem's solution.

Problem 3.11 (Grades 4–6)

In my pocket, I have quarters and nickels. I have four more nickels than quarters. Altogether, I have $1.70 in my pocket. How many nickels and how many quarters do I have?

Solution: Using the guess and test strategy:

Quarters	Value	Nickels	Value	Total Value
1	25¢	5	25¢	50¢ (Too small)
2	50¢	6	30¢	80¢ (Still too small)
3	75¢	7	35¢	$1.10 (Getting there)
4	$1.00	8	40¢	$1.40 (Better)
5	$1.25	9	45¢	$1.70 (Yes!)

Answer: I have 9 nickels and 5 quarters..

Problem 3.12 (Grades 6–7)

The local golf pro is trying to get youngsters interested in his golf program. He shares 36 golf balls among three children. He gives some to Snap, and twice as many to Crackle. He then gives Pop three times as many as he gave to Crackle. How many golf balls did each child receive?

Solution: Using the guess and test strategy with a table:

Snap	Crackle	Pop	Total
6	12	36	54 (Too many)
3	6	18	27 (Too few)
5	10	30	45 (Too many)
4	8	24	36 (Yes!)

Answer: Snap received 4 golf balls, Crackle received 8, and Pop received 24.

Teaching Notes: Some children are acquainted with algebraic techniques. For these children, the problem becomes one of solving algebraically the equation

$$x + 2x + 6x = 36$$

where

x = the number of golf balls given to Snap
$2x$ = the number given to Crackle
$6x$ = the number given to Pop.

Combining terms gives

$$9x = 36$$

and hence $x = 4$. So Snap received 4 golf balls, Crackle received 8, and Pop received 24.

Problem 3.13 (Grades 5–7)

Al is editing a new math textbook. Unfortunately, someone switched the numbers on two facing pages. The product of the two numbers is 812. What were the two numbers?

Solution: To factor a number such as 812, we can use the intelligent guess and test strategy. Here is how this might appear.

Pages	Product
25×24	600 (Too small)
31×32	992 (Too large)
27×26	702 (Too small but closer)
29×28	812 (Yes!)

Answer: The numbers of the two facing pages are 28 and 29.

Teaching Notes: This might be a good time to point out that the units digit of the product, 2, can be obtained only by multiplying 2×1, 3×4, 7×6, or 9×8. Thus the guess might be 26×27 and then 28×29.

4

Solving a Simpler Equivalent Problem

It should be apparent to you that a problem usually can be solved in more than one way. But finding a solution method often can be made more complicated by the numbers used or the context in which the problem finds itself. One simple way to make a problem more manageable and that usually yields good results is to change the given problem into an equivalent one that may be easier to solve—that is, by simplifying the numbers given in the problem. This can give the students insight into how to solve the original problem. In some cases, the simpler problem might only involve using numbers that are easier for the student to work with, but it may also be simplified by considering a simpler case of the problem. Once students have solved the simpler version, they can proceed to the original (perhaps more complex) problem.

APPLYING THE SOLVING A SIMPLER EQUIVALENT PROBLEM STRATEGY

Consider the following problem:

The divisors of 360 add up to 1,170. What is the sum of the reciprocals of the divisors of 360?

Solution. The most obvious solution would be to find all the divisors of 360, take their reciprocals, and then add. The divisors of 360 are 1, 2, 3, 4, 5, 6, 8, 9 ... 120, 180, and 360. The reciprocals are $\frac{1}{1}, \frac{1}{2}, \frac{1}{3}, \frac{1}{4}, \frac{1}{5}, \frac{1}{6}, \frac{1}{8}, \frac{1}{9} \cdots \frac{1}{120}, \frac{1}{180}, \frac{1}{360}$.

We then find a common denominator (for example, 360), convert all the fractions to their equivalents, and add. Unfortunately, it is quite easy to make a mechanical or computational error, as well as possibly miss one or more divisors.

Let's examine a simpler equivalent problem. Let's find the sum of the reciprocals of the divisors of 12 and see if this helps. The divisors of 12 are 1, 2, 3, 4, 6, and 12. Their sum is $1 + 2 + 3 + 4 + 6 + 12 = 28$. Now let's find the sum of the reciprocals of these factors:

$$\frac{1}{1} + \frac{1}{2} + \frac{1}{3} + \frac{1}{4} + \frac{1}{6} + \frac{1}{12} = \frac{12}{12} + \frac{6}{12} + \frac{4}{12} + \frac{3}{12} + \frac{2}{12} + \frac{1}{12} = \frac{28}{12}$$

Aha! The numerator of the fraction is the sum of the divisors, and the denominator is the number with which we're working. Now we can solve our original problem.

The sum of the factors of 360 is 1,170. Thus, the sum of the reciprocals of the factors must be $\frac{1170}{360}$.

CHAPTER TEACHING NOTES

This is a somewhat sophisticated problem-solving approach and, in a number of ways, among the more elegant we discuss in this book. As noted, students need to examine the structure of the problem and, holding that structure in mind, attempt a somewhat simpler problem. In the above, for example, this was accomplished by looking at the sum of the reciprocals of the factors of 12 rather than 360. Students will then need to experiment with what they perceive to be the structure of the problem—for example, in the above, you might wish to check whether the sums of the reciprocals of the factors of 24 are as expected—and, rather than generalizing the solutions, will need to generalize the solution technique.

Students often will find all this difficult. They will, understandably, attempt to use an approach they found previously effective—perhaps lists or systematic guessing. Although such approaches will, in theory, give answers to the problems we have posed, they are at best quite tedious. You will need to get students to reflect, to look for alternative and elegant strategies. This can be encouraged by modeling and by featuring student work that is efficient and elegant. However, this is largely dispositional. Once students get a taste of the elegance and power of mathematics, they will supply the motivation.

PROBLEMS FOR STUDENTS

Problem 4.1 (Grades 5–6)

A zookeeper has ostriches and elephants in one part of the zoo. Altogether the animals account for 60 heads and 180 legs. How many of each animal does he have?

Solution: We can reduce the complexity of the problem and work with a simpler but equivalent set of numbers. Divide by 10. Let's try to solve the problem for 6 heads and 18 legs. We will work with these smaller numbers, and then we will go back to the original numbers.

Ostriches have 2 legs and elephants have 4 legs. Make a drawing and represent the heads with a **0**.

0	0	0	0	0	0

Now, whether it's an elephant or an ostrich, it has *at least* 2 legs. Let's put these "*//*" on each of the heads (0).

0	0	0	0	0	0
//	//	//	//	//	//

That accounts for 12 legs. The rest go on in pairs on three of the heads.

//	//	//			
0	0	0	0	0	0
//	//	//	//	//	//

There are 3 elephants and 3 ostriches. Now multiply by 10 to find the actual answers. (Remember, we divided by 10 to get smaller numbers to work with.)

Notice that this problem also makes use of the Make a Drawing strategy. (As we have stated earlier, more than one strategy will often be used to solve a problem.)

Answer: He has 30 ostriches and 30 elephants.

Problem 4.2 (Grades 3–4)

Ian is playing a space invaders game on his computer. Every time he knocks one of the spacemen off the spaceship, he gets 3 points. Yesterday, he knocked 53 spacemen off the alien ship. Was his score an odd number or an even number?

Solution: Let's look at a simpler problem, say we have 6 spacemen instead of 53 spacemen. His score would be as follows:

Number Knocked Off the Ship	1	2	3	4	5	6
Score	3	6	9	12	15	18

Looking at the table, we see that if he knocks off an even number of spacemen (2, 4, or 6), his score is an even number. If he knocks an odd number off the ship, his score is an odd number. Because 53 is an odd number, the score must also be an odd number.

Some students may simply multiply the number of spacemen he knocked off the ship by 3 to get the actual score. Others may already know that the product of two odd numbers is an odd number, in which case this problem is inappropriate except for review.

Answer: His score is an odd number.

Problem 4.3 (Grades 5–6)

Art has 35 feet of flat oak board. He wants to make bookshelves that will be exactly 5 feet long. It takes him 2 minutes to make one cut through the board. How long will it take him to make the shelves?

Solution: Art has 35 feet of board. If each shelf is to be 5 feet long, he will make 7 shelves. We have to find out how many cuts he must make. To do this, let's look at simpler versions of the problem. Suppose Art had a board and needed to cut it into two parts. He would need 1 cut. How about cutting a board into three parts? He would need 2 cuts (see Figure 4.1).

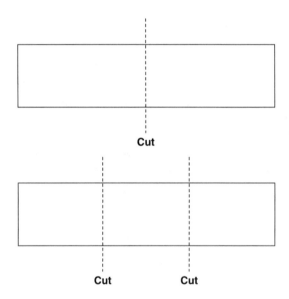

Figure 4.1

Aha! It looks like he needs one cut fewer than the number of pieces. There is a pattern to be seen. Now we can solve our problem. To make 7 shelves, Art must make 6 cuts. Because each cut takes him 2 minutes, it will take him 12 minutes to cut the shelves.

Answer: Art will take 12 minutes to cut the board into seven 5-foot shelves.

Problem 4.5 (Grades 3–5)

Ed is making a design for the floor of his basement. He is using a box with 784 square tiles to make a larger square. He wants to make the largest square possible using the 784 tiles. What are the dimensions of the largest square Ed can make?

Solution: We can try different combinations of the square tiles to see how large a square we can make. However, this is time-consuming and might not lead to the correct answer. Instead, we shall try a simpler version of the problem, by starting with a 1×1 square, then a 2×2 square, then a 3×3 square, and so on. We can keep our data in a table.

Number of Tiles on a Side	1	2	3	4	5 ...	10 ...	20 ...	25	26	27	28
Area (Total Tiles)	1	4	9	16	25 ...	100 ...	400 ...	625	676	729	784

Answer: The largest square Ed can make is 28×28. He will use all 784 tiles.

Teaching Notes: For those students who understand the concept of square root, all that needs to be done is to take the square root of 784 (using a calculator).

Problem 4.6 (Grades 3–5)

Maria has been asked to find three consecutive even numbers whose sum is 60. What are the numbers?

Solution: We use the simpler problem strategy. We begin with the smallest set of three even numbers, then try the next set, and so on, to see if there is a pattern we can make use of.

$2 + 4 + 6 = 12$	Set 1 begins with 2 (which is 1×2)
$4 + 6 + 8 = 18$	Set 2 begins with 4 (which is 2×2)
$6 + 8 + 10 = 24$	Set 3 begins with 6 (which is 3×2)
$8 + 10 + 12 = 30$	Set 4 begins with 8 (which is 4×2)

Aha! The sum is going up by 6. The sums will be 12, 18, 24, 30, 36, 42, 48, 54, and 60.

We want the 9th sum, 60. The three consecutive even numbers that give that sum will begin with 9×2, or 18. We will try $18 + 20 + 22 = 60$.

Answer: The three consecutive even numbers whose sum is 60 are 18, 20, and 22.

Teaching Notes: This problem provides practice for those students who need work in addition. They can continue adding the sequences of three consecutive numbers until they actually find all the sums and reach the required 60.

We can also show students that the sum of three consecutive even numbers is always three times the middle number. Therefore, $60/3 = 20$, which is then the middle number, gives us the three numbers $18 + 20 + 22 = 60$.

Problem 4.7 (Grades 3–5)

Maurice put 7 cubes in a row, tight against one another. Then he spray-painted them with red paint. When they had dried, he took them apart. He noticed that faces of the cube that were touching the table did not get painted, nor did the faces of cubes that touched one another. How many faces of the 7 cubes were painted?

Solution: We can reduce the number of cubes to a smaller number and see what happens. We can look for a pattern to develop.

Number of Cubes	Faces Painted
1	5
2	8
3	11

As we add one cube, the number of painted faces increases by 3. Let's complete the table.

Number of Cubes	Faces Painted
1	5
2	8
3	11
4	14
5	17
6	20
7	23

Answer: There will be 23 painted faces for 7 cubes.

Teaching Notes: Some of your students may notice that the number of faces painted can be found by multiplying the number of cubes by 3 and adding 2. This can be expressed in a number sentence format as $F = 3n + 2$, where F is the number of painted faces and n is the number of cubes. You may wish to point this out to the class.

Problem 4.8 (Grades 5–7)

Lucy has 10 pieces of candy. She and her two sisters want to divide the candy so that each of them gets at least 1 piece of candy. In how many ways can she do this?

Solution: Let us look at a simpler version of the problem. If we had 3 pieces of candy (the minimum number of pieces with all 3 children getting at least one piece), there would only be 1 way to divide the candy.

3 pieces of candy: 1–1–1	1 way
4 pieces of candy: 1–1–2, 1–2–1, 2–1–1	3 ways
5 pieces of candy: 1–1–3, 1–3–1, 3–1–1, 2–2–1, 2–1–2, 1–2–2	6 ways
6 pieces of candy: 1–1–4, 1–4–1, 4–1–1, 3–2–1, 3–1–2, 2–1–3, 2–3–1, 1–3–2, 1–2–3, 2–2–2	10 ways

We can prepare a table to show this:

Number of Pieces of Candy	3	4	5	6	7	8	9	10
Number of Ways to Divide	1	3	6	10	15	21	28	36

Continuing along with the chart, we get the required number of ways that 10 pieces of candy can be distributed.

Answer: There are 36 ways they can divide the 10 pieces of candy.

Teaching Notes: Your students may have seen these numbers before; they are called the triangular numbers because these numbers of dots can be arranged symmetrically as an equilateral triangle. If students have not seen these numbers before, you can point out to them that the difference between successive numbers increases by 1 each time—that is, between 3 and 1 is 2, between 6 and 3 is 3, between 10 and 6 is 4, and so on. In this way, they can construct the same table. The triangular numbers appear in many of the problems in this book.

Problem 4.9 (Grades 6–7)

Mrs. Edwards' class was given the following problem:

In parallelogram *ABCD*, a point, *E*, is selected anywhere on side *CD*. Line segments *AE* and *BE* are drawn as shown in Figure 4.2.

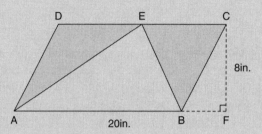

Figure 4.2

Side *AB* equals 20" and the altitude *CF* = 8".
Which has the greater area, Triangle *ABE* or Triangle *AED* + Triangle *BEC*?

Solution: Let's look at this problem and see if we can make it simpler and yet equivalent. Because the location of point *E* was not specified, other than that it must lie on *CD*, we can place it anywhere we wish. Let's move it to coincide with point *C* (see Figure 4.3).

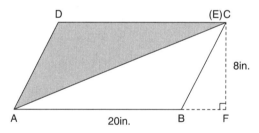

Figure 4.3

Now the two shaded triangles become one, and segment *AE* is a diagonal. Thus, the shaded triangles are half of the original parallelogram, or 40 square feet.

Some students may attempt to find the area of the three triangles. This will lead to a correct answer, but it depends on the student realizing that the bases of triangles *DEA* and *CEB* add up to the side *CD* or 20. Furthermore, the altitude of each of the three triangles = 8 because it lies between parallel line segments. Other students may find the area of the parallelogram and the area of triangle *AEB* and subtract. Either solution, although more complicated than that given above, would be correct.

Answer: The areas are the same, 40 square feet.

Teaching Notes: The concept of moving point *E* until it coincides with point *C* may be a bit difficult for some of your students to comprehend. That's fine, because either of the other two solutions would also suffice. However, for those who do understand it, this idea is well worth discussing in class.

Problem 4.10 (Grades 3–5)

Barbara wants to buy some boxes in which to store her toy soldier collection. She buys 5 large boxes. Inside each large box are two medium boxes. Inside each medium box are two small boxes. How many boxes in all did Barbara buy?

Solution: We can solve a simpler equivalent problem, by using one large box and then multiplying our answer by 5 (because we actually have to account for 5 large boxes). Let's find the number of boxes combined if we had only one large box. We can then multiply our answer by 5. One large box + 2 medium boxes + 4 small boxes = 7 boxes. Finally, $7 \times 5 = 35$.

If we combine the above solution method together with the making a drawing strategy, we can easily show one box with two medium boxes inside and two small boxes inside each medium box (see Figure 4.4). We can then count the total number of boxes, 7, and multiply by 5.

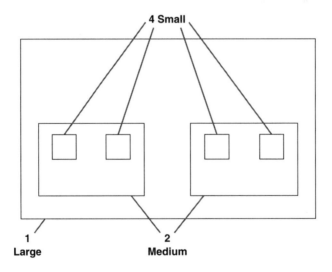

Figure 4.4

Answer: Barbara bought 35 boxes in all.

Teaching Notes: When students attempt this problem, a common error is to forget the original large boxes. You may wish to emphasize counting these boxes.

Problem 4.11 (Grades 5–7)

If 3 chickens can lay 4 eggs in 5 days, how many days will it take 12 chickens to lay 48 eggs?

Solution: Rather than consider this problem in its entirety, we solve it as a pair of simpler problems. If 3 chickens lay 4 eggs in 5 days (that is, 3 chickens = 4 eggs in 5 days), then multiplying the number of eggs and the number of chickens by 4 to gives us: 12 chickens lay 16 eggs in the same 5 days (that is, 12 chickens = 16 eggs in 5 days). To get 48 eggs, we need to multiply 16 eggs by 3. To do this we multiply the number of days and the number of eggs by 3 to get 12 chickens lay 48 eggs in 15 days.

Answer: It will take the chickens 15 days to lay 48 eggs.

Teaching Notes: The problem involves some algebraic manipulation of "relationships." That is, because 3 chickens = 4 eggs (in 5 days), multiply both sides of the "equation" by 3 and get 12 chickens = 16 eggs (in 5 days). Similarly, because 16 eggs = 5 days, we can multiply both sides of this "equation" by 3 and get 48 eggs = 15 days.

5

Acting It Out or Simulation

This strategy is especially useful in grades 3 and 4. Young children can actually take on roles from the problem and perform the action. They can also use materials such as chips, bottle caps, and so on to simulate the action in the problem. The ultimate simulation is, of course, to use numbers.

APPLYING THE ACTING IT OUT OR SIMULATION STRATEGY

The problem of estimating π—the ratio of the circumference of a circle to its diameter—is often taken up in the upper elementary grades. One solution is to measure the circumference and diameter of a circle and then to compute an approximate value for π. Such an approximation is, of course, limited to the precision of the instruments used for measurement. However, using simulation, we can, in theory, compute π to an arbitrary degree of accuracy.

Consider a circle with radius of 1 unit (see Figure 5.1).

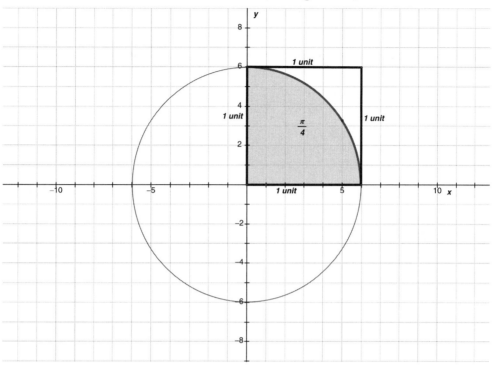

Figure 5.1

The area (πr^2) of the circle shown in Figure 5.1 is π. (Note that areas are expressed in square units.) The area of the sector (the region of the quarter circle within the square) has an area of $\frac{\pi}{4}$. So, the ratio of the area of the sector to the area of the square is $\frac{\frac{\pi}{4}}{1} = \frac{\pi}{4}$. This can also be written as

$$\pi = \frac{4 \cdot \text{Area of sector}}{\text{Area of square}}.$$

To estimate these areas and hence this ratio, we can use the areas on a coordinate graph paper. Students can estimate the area bounded the sector and compare that to the area of the square. The accuracy will depend on the size of the circle versus the size of the small squares of the graph paper.

One can take a somewhat more sophisticated approach by realizing that the points (x, y) on a circle of radius one is $x^2 + y^2 = 1$. All the points inside a circle satisfy the condition that $x^2 + y^2 < 1$. If we take a relatively small number of randomly selected points (x, y), each of which is less than 1, to make sure that it remains within the square, then $x^2 + y^2$ will tell us whether the point is inside the quarter circle or outside the quarter circle. In the chart below, the three values of $x^2 + y^2$ marked with an asterisk are outside the circle, leaving 17 points inside the circle. From this small set of randomly selected data, we can approximate $\pi \approx \dfrac{4 \times 17}{20} = 3.4$.

This rough approximation of π is based on a relatively small sample of points, but it will allow students to simulate a procedure, which can give solid insight into a mathematical concept.

(x, y)	$x^2 + y^2$
(0.75, 0.64)	0.9721
(0.24, 0.05)	0.0601
(0.63, 0.18)	0.4293
(0.38, 0.81)	0.8005
(0.25, 0.59)	0.4106
(0.12, 0.28)	0.0928
(0.36, 0.59)	0.4777
(0.91, 0.72)	1.34650*
(0.86, 0.04)	0.7412
(0.01, 0.05)	0.0026
(0.26, 0.95)	0.9701
(0.45, 0.27)	0.2754
(0.74, 0.07)	0.5525
(0.77, 0.99)	1.57300*
(0.45, 0.65)	0.6250
(0.77, 0.53)	0.0293
(0.95, 0.11)	0.9140
(0.29, 0.40)	0.2441
(0.79, 0.14)	0.9050
(0.75, 0.73)	1.09540*

CHAPTER TEACHING NOTES

The strategy of simulation is akin to what has been termed *real-world* problem solving. That is, students are encouraged to use their developing mathematics skills to solve problems within contexts of situations they find familiar. However, such familiarity cannot be taken for granted as students bring different experiences to the classroom. Thus, some time—and this is the drawback to all real-world problem solving—must be taken, prior to independent work on a problem, to discuss its context and purpose.

The problems in this chapter have been chosen so that there often exist several equally valid and efficient solutions. Students should be encouraged to share and discuss each other's solutions. You may want to formalize such communication with individual or group presentations. In any case, as we have noted previously, you should encourage creativity and elegance, and at the same time require that students approach a problem systematically. These are not problems to be solved by brute arithmetic calculation, but through formulating plans and choosing effective strategies.

PROBLEMS FOR STUDENTS

Problem 5.1 (Grades 3–5)

Distribute Cuisenaire rods for this problem. The rods are the cars of a train. Each rod (car) holds the same number of people as its length. Thus:

| 1 = **White** | 2 = **Red** | 3 = **Green** | 4 = **Violet** | 5 = **Yellow** |

You have one rod of each color and length. Show how you can build a train of lengths from 1 through 15.

Solution: Many of these trains can be done in more than one way. (Only some are shown.)

1 = W	6 = W + Y or R + V	11 = Y + V + R
2 = R	7 = V + G or Y + R	12 = Y + V + G
3 = G	8 = Y + G or V + G + W	13 = Y + V + G + W
4 = V	9 = Y + V	14 = Y + V + G + R
5 = Y	10 = Y + V + W	15 = Y + V + G + R + W

Students should be encouraged to find alternate ways to represent the various lengths. Those students who find this easy might be asked about how many ways each of these lengths can be represented.

Answer: As shown above.

Problem 5.2 (Grades 3–4)

The new sports shop sent out 40 coupons, each one good for a free T-shirt. At the end of the day, they had given away 2 T-shirts for every 5 coupons they had sent. How many T-shirts did they give away?

Solution: The problem can be solved arithmetically. If we divide the 40 coupons by 5, we find that there are 8 groups of 5. Because each group gets 2 T-shirts, there will be 8×2 or 16 T-shirts given away. However, this method requires multiplication and division, with which the students may not be properly experienced.

Alternatively, you can have the students act out the problem. Simulate the action by letting chips stand for the coupons. Give each group of students 40 chips and have them arrange them in groups of 5 until all 40 chips have been grouped.

| ///// | ///// | ///// | ///// | ///// | ///// | ///// | ///// |

Two of every five were traded in for T-shirts. There are 8 groups of 5; there will be 8 groups of 2 T-shirts. Take out the 2 chips from each group and count the result.

Answer: There were 16 coupons redeemed for T-shirts.

Problem 5.3 (Grades 3–5)

Mr. Perlman is giving the 19 goldfish from the science lab to three students to care for during the summer. Each student gets an odd number of goldfish. Jack gets the most, Sam gets the smallest number, and Max gets the rest. How many goldfish did each of them take home to care for?

Solution: An elegant method is to give the children 19 slips of paper or 19 chips to represent the goldfish. Have them act out the problem. The only sets of three different odd numbers that add up to 19 are {3, 7, 9}, {3, 5, 11}, {1, 5, 13}, and {1, 7, 11}.

Answer: Jack got 9 goldfish to take care of, Max got 7, and Sam got 3; Jack got 11, Max got 5, and Sam got 3; Jack got 13, Max got 5, and Sam got 1; or Jack got 11, Max got 7, and Sam got 1.

Problem 5.4 (Grades 3–6)

Sharon and Janet counted the number of baseball cards they have together. They have a total of 16 baseball cards. Which of the following statements **cannot** be true and why?

(a) Janet has 13 cards.

(b) Sharon has 12 cards.

(c) Janet has 1 more card than Sharon.

(d) Sharon has 2 more cards than Janet.

(e) Sharon has an odd number of cards.

(f) Janet has an even number of cards.

Solution: Give the children 16 chips or slips of paper and have them try each of the given statements to see if it can be true. They can try to "act out" each of the possible answers and then come to the conclusion that statement (c) is impossible.

Teaching Notes: You might go a little deeper into the mathematics taken up in this activity by noting that if Janet had 1 more than Sharon, then one of them would have an odd number of cards and the other would have an even number of cards. The sum of an odd and an even number is always an odd number. Therefore (c) is impossible, because 16 is not an odd number.

Answer: Statement (c) cannot be true.

Problem 5.5 (Grades 3–6)

How many different towers, 4 blocks high, can be made from blocks of 2 different colors?

Solution: Use Unifix cubes or actual blocks for students to act out what is called for in the problem. Give each student (or group of students) 4 blocks of each of two different colors; for example, red and green. Have them actually make the towers and keep track using a system similar to that below:

R	R	R	R	G		R	R	R
R	R	R	G	R		R	G	G
R	R	G	R	R		G	R	G
R	G	R	R	R		G	G	R

R	G	G	G		G	G	G		G
G	R	G	G		R	G	R		G
G	G	R	G		R	R	G		G
G	G	G	R		G	R	R		G

In the upper elementary grades, you may want to introduce the multiplication principle (see Chapter 10, Problem 10.1 for further discussion). That is, students are asked to determine the number of ways to fill the bottom block (2, a red or a green block), and the number of ways to fill each of the next three blocks (each in 2 ways), and then, after some discussion of the multiplication principle, find they can multiply to get $2 \times 2 \times 2 \times 2$ to obtain 16 possible towers.

Answer: There are 16 possible towers that can be built.

Problem 5.6 (Grades: 3–4)

Rona is shorter than Tess but taller than Samantha. Una is shorter than Vera but taller than Tess. Who is the tallest and who is the shortest of the 5 girls?

Solution: Select 5 students to represent Rona, Samantha, Tess, Una and Vera. Then have these students actually line up according to the information given in the problem. They will move around as the problem develops. The final order is Vera tallest, then Una, Tess, Rona, and Samantha.

Answer: Vera is the tallest and Samantha is the shortest.

Teaching Notes: Some students may solve this problem by drawing a picture. Students should be encouraged to pursue various solution paths when appropriate. Discuss each solution with the class.

Problem 5.7 (Grades 3–5)

There are 18 blocks in three unequal stacks. The first stack has 3 more blocks than the third stack. The third stack has 6 fewer blocks than the second stack. How many blocks are in each stack?

Solution: Students should take 18 blocks (or any other entities, such as paper squares) and act out the problem.

Answer: The first stack has 6 blocks, the second has 9 blocks, and the third has 3 blocks.

Problem 5.8 (Grades 3–5)

Brunhilde's mother brought a sheet of 24 stamps home from the post office (see Figure 5.2). Brunhilde needed three stamps from the sheet, and so she tore out three connected stamps. How many different shape arrangements of the three stamps are possible?

Figure 5.2

Solution: Students should be encouraged to take 3 small square tiles, simulate the action, and see how many different shape arrangements of 3 attached stamps they can make (see Figure 5.3).

Figure 5.3

Answer: There are 6 different arrangements of the 3 stamps that Brunhilde can make.

Teaching Notes: Ask the students how they know when they have made all possible arrangements of the 3 stamps. They should see that they have arranged the squares in all possible ways.

Problem 5.9 (Grades 5–7)

Mom baked a cake and put it in the refrigerator. Dad came along and ate $\frac{1}{6}$ of the cake. Later, Sam came along and ate $\frac{1}{5}$ of what was left. Later, Susan ate $\frac{1}{4}$ of what was left. That evening, Mitchell ate $\frac{1}{3}$ of what was left. Arnell, the baby, ate $\frac{1}{2}$ of what was left, and mom finally got to eat the rest of the cake. Who ate the most cake?

Solution: Let's act out the problem.

- Let's begin with 6 equal size pieces of paper to simulate the entire cake.
- Dad eats $\frac{1}{6}$, which leaves 5 equal pieces (or $\frac{5}{6}$ of the cake).
- Sam eats $\frac{1}{5}$, which leaves 4 equal pieces (notice that Sam's $\frac{1}{5}$ is the same size as dad's $\frac{1}{6}$; the remaining 4 pieces represent $\frac{4}{6}$ of the cake).
- Susan eats $\frac{1}{4}$, which leaves 3 equal pieces (again, her $\frac{1}{4}$ is the same size as the other pieces).
- Mitchell eats $\frac{1}{3}$ of the pieces, which leaves 2 equal pieces.
- Arnell eats 1 of the remaining 2 pieces, leaving 1 equal-size piece.
- Mom eats the remaining piece of cake.

Notice that although the fractions are different, each person ate the same amount of cake. This is a great place to point out that a fraction must represent a part of something—it does not stand alone. In this problem, each person was taking a fractional part of a different number of pieces.

Answer: Everyone ate the same size piece of cake, namely $\frac{1}{6}$ of the cake.

Problem 5.10 (Grades 3–5)

Marcus, Nina, and Ophelia were hunting Easter eggs. Ophelia found 15 eggs. Nina found 7 fewer than Marcus. Ophelia found 5 more than Nina. How many Easter eggs did the three children find altogether?

Solution: Use a pack of chips or blocks to represent the Easter eggs and actually act it out or simulate the action. Pick three children to represent Marcus, Nina, and Ophelia. Start by giving Ophelia 15 chips. This is 5 more than Nina, so give Nina 10 chips. Nina found 7 fewer than Marcus, so Marcus must have 17 chips.

Answer: Together, the children found 17 + 10 + 15 = 42 Easter eggs.

Problem 5.11 (Grades 3–5)

Max has three stacks of blocks with numbers on them as shown in Figure 5.4. He claims that he can make the sums of the numbers on all three stacks equal the same amount by moving just one block. How can Max do it?

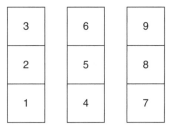

Figure 5.4

Solution: Get 9 blocks and paste a slip of paper on each with the number as shown. Students can now physically move the blocks around to see when the sums are the same in all three stacks. A little bit of logical reasoning can help. Because the sum of all 9 numbers is 45, and there are three equal stacks, each stack must total 45 ÷ 3 = 15. The middle stack already has a sum of 15, so the block to be moved must come from the other two stacks. Furthermore, because the first stack only adds up to 6, the block must come from the third stack. In fact, moving the blocks from stack #3 one at a time to stack #1 will reveal the correct answer.

Answer: Move the "9" block from stack #3 to stack #1. Now all three stacks have a sum of 15.

Problem 5.12 (Grades 3–5)

Senta has 16 mineral rocks in her collection. She wants to put them on display in the school showcase. She arranges them so that there are the same number of rocks in each row. In how many ways can she do this?

Solution: Take 16 chips and arrange them in all possible ways in equal rows (see Figure 5.5).

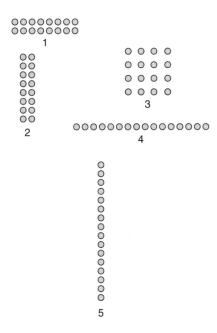

Figure 5.5

Answer: There are 5 different ways she can arrange the rocks:

2 rows of 8, 8 rows of 2, 4 rows of 4, 16 rows of 1, 1 row of 16.

Teaching Notes: This might be a good time to discuss the fact that 8 rows of 2 are different from 2 rows of 8—even though they are *companions*. You might also point out that 4×4 is unique; that is, it has no *companion* arrangement. If we had 9 rocks, for example, then we could arrange them as 1×9 or 9×1. However, there would be a single 3×3 arrangement with no *companion*. This could be used to develop the concept of a perfect square.

6

Working Backwards

This strategy can be difficult for the students to master. For most of their mathematical lives, they have been taught to start at the beginning of a problem and carry the action through, on a step-by-step basis. The "Working Backwards" strategy, however, takes the opposite turn. The students begin with the end result of the problem, and carry the action backwards to find conditions at the beginning. The mathematical operations are reversed; so, for example, what was subtraction now becomes the inverse operation, namely, addition.

Once the answer has been found, the results can be checked by starting with this answer and carrying the action through from start to finish. This is the one strategy that "advertises" itself by stating the end conditions of the problem and asking to find the starting conditions.

Although, on the surface, the procedure may seem unnatural, it is used in everyday decision making without much fanfare. Take, for example, the task of finding the best route to an unfamiliar place on a map. Typically, we first try to locate the destination point and then gradually work backwards through a network of roads until we get to familiar surroundings. However, when it comes to mathematical applications of this technique, we have to encourage students to include this procedure in their arsenal of problem-solving tools, even where it may not be in an obvious problem-solving technique.

APPLYING THE WORKING BACKWARDS STRATEGY

Consider the following problem:

Evelyn, Henry, and Al play a certain game. The player who loses each round must give each of the other players as much money as each of them has at that time. In Round 1, Evelyn loses and gives Henry and Al as much money as they each have. In Round 2, Henry loses, and gives Evelyn and Al as much money as they each then have. Al loses in Round 3 and gives Evelyn and Henry as much money as they each have. They decide to quit at this point and discover that they each have $24. How much money did they each start with?

Solution: You may have begun this problem by setting up a system of three equations in three variables. Can it be done? Of course! However, because the problem requires a great deal of subtraction and simplification of parenthetical expressions, the final set of equations stands the chance of being incorrect. Even if the correct set of equations is obtained, it must then be solved simultaneously:

Round	Evelyn	Henry	Al
Start	x	y	z
1	$x - y - z$	$2y$	$2z$
2	$2x - 2y - 2z$	$3y - x - z$	$4z$
3	$4x - 4y - 4z$	$6y - 2x - 2z$	$7z - x - y$

This leads us to the following system of equations:

$$4x - 4y - 4z = 24,$$
$$-2x + 6y - 2z = 24,$$
$$-x - y + 7z = 24$$

Solving the system leads to $x = 39$, $y = 21$, and $z = 12$. Thus, Evelyn began with $39, Henry began with $21, and Al began with $12.

When a problem states its situation at the end of the story ("They each have $24") and asks for the starting situation ("How much money did they each start with?"), this is almost a sure sign that the **working backwards**

strategy could be employed. Let's see how this makes our work easier. We begin at the end with each having $24:

	Evelyn	Henry	Al
End of Round 3	24	24	24
End of Round 2	12	12	48
End of Round 1	6	42	24
Start	39	21	12

End of Round 2: Because Al loses in Round 3, Evelyn and Henry double what they have in Round 2. Thus at the end of Round 2, Evelyn and Henry each had $12 and Al had $48 = $24 + $12 + $12.

End of Round 1: Because Henry loses in Round 2, Evelyn and Al double what they had in Round 1. Thus at the end of Round 1, Evelyn had $6, Al had $24, and Henry had $12 + $6 + $24 = $42.

Start: Because Evelyn loses in Round 1, Henry and Al double what they had at the start. Thus, at the start, Henry had $21, Al had $12, and Evelyn had $6 + $21 + $12 = $39.

These are the same answers we arrived at by solving the problem algebraically.

CHAPTER TEACHING NOTES

As we have noted previously, it is important to give yourself and your students opportunities to discuss their thinking about a problem before they begin independent work. This is fundamental to using this strategy. Students must have a reasonable grasp of the structure of a problem prior to being able to trace the problem from the ending conditions back to the starting point. In particular, it is essential that students are able, once they determine a set of starting conditions, to check their answer.

Such discussion might usefully include mention of analogous computational exercises they have previously mastered. You might focus on similarities and ask students to look for clues. As always, students should be encouraged to plan their mathematics efforts and look for elegant and efficient solutions.

PROBLEMS FOR STUDENTS

Problem 6.1 (Grades 4–6)

Ilana, Jennie, Karl, and Luis are members of the school stamp club. Last week, they traded stamps. When the meeting was over and they had finished trading, Ilana had 28 stamps. She had given 10 to Jennie, and she received 12 from Karl and 7 from Luis. How many stamps did Ilana start with?

Solution: Because we know how many stamps Ilana finished with (the end condition) and want to know what she started with (the beginning condition), we can use the working backwards strategy.

Ilana finished with 28.	She had 28.
She got 7 from Luis.	She must have previously had 21.
She got 12 from Karl.	She must have previously had 9.
She gave Jennie 10.	She must have started with 19.

Answer: She started with 19 stamps.

Teaching Notes: To check the answer, begin at the beginning with 19 stamps and follow the action from start to finish. You should end up with Ilana having 28 stamps.

Problem 6.2 (Grades 5–7)

Happy Harry, the new disc jockey, is planning his Saturday evening program. It's a one-hour program, but he must allow 5 minutes for news, 4 minutes for weather, 3 minutes for local announcements, and 27 minutes for commercials. If each song he plays averages 3 minutes, how many songs can he plan for his Saturday evening program?

Solution: Because we know the end of the problem (1 hour) and want to find the earlier information, we can use the working backwards strategy.

Total time	60 minutes
News	*– 5 minutes*
	55 minutes
Weather	*– 4 minutes*
	51 minutes
Local announcements	*– 3 minutes*
	48 minutes
Commercials	*– 27 minutes*
Songs	21 minutes

Because each song averages 3 minutes, he can play 21 ÷ 3 = 7 songs.

Answer: He can play 7 songs in one hour.

Teaching Notes: Again, work forward as a check. Begin with 21 minutes of songs. Add 27 minutes for commercials, 3 minutes for local announcements, 4 minutes for weather, and 5 minutes for news. The total should be 60 minutes.

Problem 6.3 (Grades 4–5)

Ron has twice the number of baseball cards as Stan. Stan has 9 more cards than Tara. Tara has 17 cards. How many baseball cards do the three friends have together?

Solution: We know the end of the problem: Tara has 17 cards. We can begin there and work backwards as follows. Tara has 17 cards. Stan has 9 more than she does, so he has 17 + 9 = 26 cards. Ron has two times the number of cards that Stan has, so he has 52 cards. Together, the three of them have 17 + 26 + 52 = 95 cards.

Answer: They have a total of 95 cards.

Problem 6.4 (Grades 5–7)

There was a jar of chocolate chip cookies on the table. Jamea and Monea were very hungry because they hadn't had anything to eat since breakfast, so they ate half the cookies. Then Victor came along and noticed the cookies. He ate a third of what was left in the jar. Shawanna, who was waiting around nearby, decided to take a fourth of the cookies left in the jar. Then Tiffany came rushing up and took one cookie to munch on in her class. When Valerie looked at the cookie jar, she saw there were two cookies left. "How many cookies were in the jar to begin with?" She asked Jennifer, who had seen the whole thing. Can you answer Valerie?

Solution: Because we know the ending of the problem (2 cookies left) and we want to find the starting situation (how many cookies were in the jar), the working backwards strategy is one we might find useful.

- Valerie saw 2 cookies in the jar at the end.
- Tiffany took one cookie. Therefore, 3 cookies must have been in the jar when she arrived.
- Shawanna took $\frac{1}{4}$ of the cookies. Therefore, 4 cookies must have been in the jar when she arrived—that is, she took one cookie.
- Victor ate $\frac{1}{3}$ of the cookies. Therefore, 6 cookies must have been in the jar when he arrived, so when he took $\frac{1}{3}$ of the cookies (2), he left 4 in the jar.
- Jamea and Monea ate half of the cookies. Therefore, there must have been double the number of cookies in the jar when they arrived, or 12 cookies.

Answer: There were 12 cookies in the cookie jar at the start.

Problem 6.5 (Grades 5–7)

The Wolverines baseball team opened a new box of baseballs for today's game. They sent $\frac{1}{3}$ of their baseballs to be rubbed with special mud to take the gloss off. They gave 15 more baseballs to their star outfielder to autograph. The batboy took 20 baseballs for batting practice. They had only 15 baseballs left. How many baseballs were in the box at the start?

Solution: We know the condition at the end of the problem ("they had 15 baseballs left") and we wish to find the number of baseballs with which the team started. This is a working backwards problem.

- They finished with 15 baseballs.
- The batboy took 20 baseballs, so they must have had 35 baseballs before that.
- They gave 15 baseballs to the star outfielder, so they must have had 50 baseballs before that.
- They sent $\frac{1}{3}$ to be rubbed, so they must have had 75 baseballs to start with, because 50 represents two-thirds, and 25 is the $\frac{1}{3}$ that was taken away.

Answer: They started with 75 baseballs.

Problem 6.6 (Grades 6–7)

You wish to boil an egg for exactly 15 minutes. The problem is, however, you only have a 7-minute timer and an 11-minute timer. How can you boil the egg for exactly 15 minutes using only these two timers?

Solution: The strategy here is to work backwards. Neither egg timer alone can time the egg for 15 minutes. Running the 7-minute timer twice consecutively will only give you 14 minutes of timing. The 11-minute timer is still missing 4 minutes to reach the desired 15 minutes. How might we measure (or time) 4 minutes that could be added on to the 11-minute timer? Turn both timers over at the same time and let them run. When the 7-minute timer is finished, there will be exactly 4 minutes left on the 11-minute timer. This is when you start your timing of the egg boiling. When the 11-minute timer runs out, turn it over and continue boiling the egg. When the 11-minute timer runs out this time, the egg has boiled for 4 + 11 = 15 minutes.

Answer: See above.

Problem 6.7 (Grades 5–7)

Roberto has a bag full of pieces of candy. As he is walking home, he meets his friend Yehor. He gives Yehor half of what he has and then gives him one extra. He walks on a little further and meets Rochelle. He gives her half of what he now has, and then one extra. Walking a little further, he comes upon a child crying. He gives him half of what he has, and one extra. When he gets home, he looks in the bag and sees that he has five pieces of candy left. How many did he start with?

Solution: Because we know the ending of the problem and wish to find out how many pieces of candy he had at the beginning, we can use the working backwards strategy. Roberto ends up with 5 pieces of candy. However he gave the crying child half of what he had and one extra. Thus, he gave him 5 + 1 or 6, so he had 12 pieces of candy at that point. When he met Rochelle, he gave her half of what he had plus an extra, so he must have had 26 (half is 13, plus 1 is 14, and 26 − 14 = 12). So, at that point, he had 26. Now, he gave half of what he had plus one extra when he met Yehor. So, at that point, he had 54 (half is 27, plus one extra is 28, and 54 − 28 = 26). Thus, Roberto started with 54 pieces of candy in the bag.

Answer: Roberto started with 54 pieces of candy.

Teaching Notes: We can check the answer by starting with 54 pieces of candy and working forward. Roberto starts with 54 pieces of candy. He meets Yehor, gives him half (27) plus one extra or 28. Thus, 54 − 28 leaves him with 26. He meets Rochelle and gives her half (13, plus an extra or 14), leaving him with 12. He meets the crying child and gives him half (6 plus an extra, or 7) leaving him with 5. Hence, our answer is correct.

Problem 6.8 (Grades 5–7)

There are 4 astronauts in a space capsule orbiting the earth. Each of them ate one food pack for breakfast, one for lunch, and one for dinner on each of the first two days. That evening, by mistake, someone dumped half of what food was left into space. When they woke up the next morning, they each had one pack for breakfast. They counted and found only 5 food packs left. How many food packs had they started with?

Solution: Let's try to work backwards.

Packs	
5	Number left
+ 4	Ate for breakfast on Day 3
9	Half that were left after dumping
+ 9	Half that were dumped
18	Amount after Day 2
+ 24	Eaten by all 4 on Days 1 and 2 ($4 \times 3 \times 2$)
42	Number started with

Answer: The astronauts started with 42 food packs.

Problem 6.9 (Grades 5–7)

Jack took 11 math tests this semester, and his average (mean) score is 75. His teacher decided that each student could drop his or her lowest test score and then the teacher would compute their averages over again. Jack dropped the 25 he had scored on one test. What would be his new average?

Solution: Let's use the working backwards strategy. To compute an average or mean, we add all the scores and divide by the number of scores. Because Jack's average for 11 tests is 75, his total before dividing must be $75 \times 11 = 825$. Let's subtract the 25 score Jack is dropping. The new total is 800 with only 10 tests. Thus, his new average is $800 \div 10 = 80$.

Answer: His new average would be 80.

Problem 6.10 (Grades 3–4)

Sam is saving to buy an electronic remote for his Speedo cars. He checked the price on January 1. He checked again in April, and it was now $6.00 higher than in January. He finally bought it in July, and it was twice as high as it had been in April; it was $52.00. How much would he have saved if he had bought it in January?

Solution: Let's work backwards.

July: $52.00	$52.00
April: half as much as July	$26.00
January: $6 less than April	$20.00

He would have saved $52.00 − $20.00 = $32.00.

Answer: He would have saved $32.00 if he had bought it in January.

Problem 6.11 (Grades 4–6)

Doug is working on a math problem in class. By mistake, he multiplies by 10 then divides by 5 instead of multiplying by 5 and then dividing by 10. If the incorrect answer he got was 3, what is the correct answer?

Solution: We must first find the original number with which Doug started. The working backwards method will be useful here.

Doug ended up with 3 after dividing by 5, so he must have had 15 at that point. He got 15 when he multiplied by 10, so he must have begun with 1.5. Now, we will work forward from 1.5 using the correct operations.

$$1.5 \times 5 = 7.5$$
$$7.5 \div 10 = 0.75$$

Answer: The correct answer is 0.75.

Problem 6.12 (Grades 5–7)

Martha stopped at the bank and took out some money. She left an envelope with the money in it on the kitchen table. On his way to work, Stu took half the money. An hour later, Rich needed some money so he took half the money that was in the envelope. Later, Ed took half the money that was in the envelope when he left the house. When Martha came home, she found $10 in the envelope. How much money had been in the envelope at the start?

Solution: Let's work backward from the amount that remains at the end of the day to figure out how much was in the envelope at the beginning of the day. Because Ed left $10 in the envelope, he must have taken $10. So, there was $20 in the envelope before he got to it. When Rich saw the envelope, it must have held exactly $40 (twice 20 dollars). He would have taken half, or $20, and left half, $20. Similarly, Stu would have seen twice this $40, or $80 in the envelope. He took $40 and left $40.

Answer: There was $80 in the envelope to start.

Problem 6.13 (Grades 3–5)

The four children in the Barnes family decided to have a surprise party for their dad. Lucy paid $12 for paper plates and cups. Mark spent $10 for the decorations. Neville spent $8 on apple juice. Olivia bought the cake for $10. To share the costs equally, how much money should each child give to the others?

Solution: We can work backwards by first determining what each person had to pay by finding the total amount required and then dividing by the number of participants.

The total spent on the party was $12 + $10 + $10 + $8 = $40. Because there are 4 children, $40 ÷ 4 = $10. Each child should pay $10.

Now we can examine what each child spent and decide who owes money to whom. Mark and Olivia have each spent exactly $10. Neville should give Lucy $10 – $8 = $2.

Answer: Neville should give Lucy $2.00.

Teaching Notes: This might be an excellent time to discuss with the students how to make a problem simpler by breaking it up into its parts and solving each part separately.

7

Finding a Pattern

A famous mathematician once said that mathematics is a search for patterns. Patterns occur in many situations. Students need practice in examining data to see if a pattern exists. Some problems will actually state that a pattern exists in a sequence of numbers and ask the student to find the pattern and/or continue the sequence for an additional few terms. Other problems may require a table or list to organize the data and see if a pattern emerges. However, a very powerful problem-solving strategy for problems that do not directly call for finding a pattern is, in fact, to search for a pattern and then use it to solve the problem.

In everyday life situations, we are often called on to find a pattern to solve a problem, but not asked to do so directly. Take, for example, searching for a particular address in a neighborhood with which you are not familiar. If you are looking for 523 Main Street, you first determine on which side are the odd-numbered addresses, and then in which order the numbers are ascending or descending. This involves finding the pattern and then continuing it to your goal. Finding a pattern can sometimes be quite challenging, whereas at other times, it is almost directly presented to you. The best way for students to learn to discover patterns is to practice finding patterns in different problem situations.

APPLYING THE FINDING A PATTERN STRATEGY

Consider the following problem:

> We have a function machine that operates only on the given number and no other. Thus, if we input 3, the machine can only operate on 3s. The machine uses the four fundamental operations of arithmetic (addition, subtraction, multiplication, and division) either alone or in combination. Here are the first five outputs for inputs of $x = 1$ through 5:

Input (x)	Output
1	1
2	9
3	29
4	67
5	129
6	221

What is the value if we input 9?

Solution: You may have begun this problem by attempting to guess the function rule. This is a very difficult and time-consuming task. However, the problem can be solved by using the **finding a pattern strategy** together with some reasoning to determine what the function machine is doing when we input a number. The output appears to be close to the cube of the input number. That is,

Input (x)	Output	x^3	Difference (from x^3)
1	1	1	0
2	9	8	+ 1 or (2–1)
3	29	27	+ 2 or (3–1)
4	67	64	+ 3 or (4–1)
5	129	125	+ 4 or (5–1)
6	221	216	+ 5 or (6–1)
•	•	•	•
•	•	•	•
•	•	•	•
x		x^3	+ (x–1)

However, because our output can contain only the input number, we must express x^3 as $x \cdot x \cdot x$ and $(x-1)$ as $(x - \frac{x}{x})$. Thus, our output rule for an input of x seems to be $x \cdot x \cdot x + x - (x - \frac{x}{x})$, and the answer to our problem is $9 \cdot 9 \cdot 9 + (9 - \frac{9}{9}) = 9^3 + 8 = 729 + 8 = 737$.

CHAPTER TEACHING NOTES

In order to effectively utilize geometric and numeric patterns in problem solving, your students need to

1. Understand the purpose for and context of the pattern. *Example:* In the above problem, understanding that we are looking for a pattern that describes the mathematical relationship between input and output.

2. Identify the repeating elements in the pattern. *Example:* In the above problem, noticing that the output values are near the cubes of the input.

3. Extend the identified pattern. *Example:* In the above problem, conjecturing that an input x gives as output $x^3 + (x–1)$.

Although such skills have their roots in the primary grades, they are continuing to be developed in grades 3 through 5. In addition to continued and varied exploration of patterns—such as offered in this chapter—your students need to learn to first notice and to then systematically organize their observations. Much of this can be addressed in class discussions prior to and subsequent to students beginning independent work. Multiple student descriptions will lay the groundwork for exploring how a pattern might be continued. Multiple student solutions will allow you to address both efficiency and elegance. Keep in mind, however, that noticing and extending only provide an outline for solving the problem. Your students must still use their conceptual understandings and computational skills to create a solution.

PROBLEMS FOR STUDENTS

Problem 7.1 (Grades 5–6)

Find the next two terms in the sequence

5, 11, 23, 47, . . .

Solution: The pattern for each term after the first in this sequence is to double the previous term and add 1. Thus the sequence is:

$5 = 5$
$2(5) + 1 = 10 + 1 = 11$
$2(11) + 1 = 22 + 1 = 23$
$2(23) + 1 = 46 + 1 = 47$
$2(47) + 1 = 94 + 1 = 95$
$2(95) + 1 = 190 + 1 = 191$
(Algebraically, the formula for any term is $2n + 1$ where n is the previous term.)

Some students may recognize a pattern of add 6, add 12, add 24, and so on. Thus, the fifth term is found by adding 48: $48 + 47 = 95$. The next term is found by adding 96: $95 + 96 = 191$. Either pattern rule is fine to solve the problem. Remember, many mathematics problems have more than one method of solution. It is good to provide students with alternate solutions, because each one increases their problem-solving fluency.

Answer: The next two terms are 95 and 191.

Problem 7.2 (Grades 4–5)

Mark is cutting circles from cardboard to make a poster for the backdrop in the school play. The diameter of the first circle is 6 cm. The diameter of the next circle is 5.5 cm, the next 5 cm. He continues in this manner, cutting circles, and his final circle has a diameter of 2.5 cm. How many circles did he cut out from the cardboard?

Solution: We examine the data, looking for a pattern. The pattern rule tells us that each circle is 0.5 cm smaller than the previous one. Let's make a table to organize the data, then follow the pattern:

Circle #	1	2	3	4	5	6	7	8
Diameter Size	6	5.5	5	4.5	4	3.5	3	2.5

He reaches a circle of diameter 2.5 at the eighth circle.

Answer: He cut 8 circles from the cardboard.

Problem 7.3 (Grades 4–6)

Mr. Evans is designing square swimming pools. Each pool has a square center that is the area of the water. Mr. Evans uses blue tiles to show the water. Around the square pool, he puts a border of white tiles. Figure 7.1 shows pictures of the three smallest pools he can design:

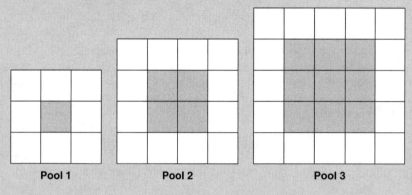

Pool 1   Pool 2   Pool 3

Figure 7.1

How many white tiles will there be in a pool that has 25 blue tiles?

Solution: Let's organize the data and see if a pattern emerges.

Pool #	Blue Tiles	White Tiles
1	$1 \times 1 = 1$	8
2	$2 \times 2 = 4$	12
3	$3 \times 3 = 9$	16

Aha! Each time the number of blue tiles increases to the next perfect square, the number of white tiles increases by 4. Continue the table.

4	$4 \times 4 = 16$	20
5	$5 \times 5 = 25$	24

This leads to our answer.

Some students may notice that the number of white tiles is the same as the perimeter of the square made up of the blue tiles plus the 4 tiles needed for each corner.

Answer: There are 24 white squares in the pool that has 25 blue tiles.

Problem 7.4 (Grades 6–8)

A regular hexagon has each side of length 1" (Figure 7.2). Two hexagons placed side by side as shown in Figure 7.3 have a perimeter of 10" (the darkened line). Three hexagons placed side by side have a perimeter of 14" (the darkened line in Figure 7.4).

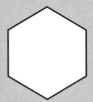

Figure 7.2

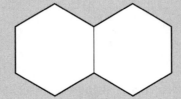

Figure 7.3

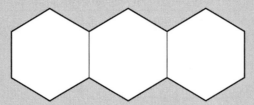

Figure 7.4

What would be the perimeter of the figure formed by 6 hexagons placed side by side in the same manner?

Solution: Let's see if we can discover a pattern each time we add a hexagon to the previous ones. If there is such a pattern we can use it to solve the problem for any number of hexagons.

Number of Hexagons	Perimeter
1	6"
2	10"
3	14"

The perimeter seems to increase by 4 as the number of hexagons increases by 1. Continue the table.

Number of Hexagons	Perimeter
1	6"
2	10"
3	14"
4	18"
5	22"
6	26"

We now have the number of tiles for 6 hexagons.

Some of your students might notice that the perimeter is equal to the number of hexagons multiplied by 4 and add 2, or, algebraically, $P = 4H + 2$.

Answer: The perimeter of a figure formed by 6 hexagons placed side by side is 26.

Teaching Notes: The problem could be made more visual using hexagonal pattern blocks. Students might also notice a pattern: There are four sides on each of the hexagons when they are placed end to end and always two sides on the ends. Algebraically, this can be represented as $4H + 2$.

Problem 7.5 (Grades 3–6)

What are the next two numbers in the sequence 2, 3, 5, 7, 11, 13, 17, . . . ?

Solution: If we look at these numbers we should be able to recognize a pattern of a different sort; namely, these are consecutive prime numbers—that is, numbers that can be divided only by themselves and 1. Therefore, the next two prime numbers are 19 and 23.

Answer: 19 and 23.

Problem 7.6 (Grades 3–5)

A standard traffic light turns green then yellow then red, then green and so on. What color is the 13th light?

Solution: The sequence of lights is green, yellow, red, green, yellow. . . . Let's make a table and follow this pattern.

Light #	1	2	3	4	5	6	7	8	9	10	11	12	13	14	15
Color	g	y	r	g	y	r	g	y	r	g	y	r	g	y	r

The 13th light would be green. Notice that the sequence of green lights is 1, 4, 7, 10, **13**, . . .

Answer: The 13th light is green.

Problem 7.7 (Grades 5–7)

A string is laid out to form a large "C" as shown in Figure 7.5. When we cut it with a single vertical line, we get 3 pieces. When we cut it with two vertical lines, we get 5 pieces. When we cut it with three vertical lines, we get 7 pieces. Into how many pieces will 7 vertical lines divide the C?

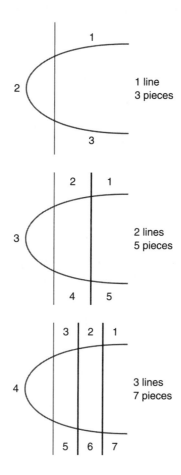

Figure 7.5

Solution: Let's make a table of what we know and see if any pattern develops.

Number of cuts	1	2	3	4	5	6	7
Number of pieces	3	5	7				

There is a pattern. Each time we add a cut, the number of pieces increases by 2. Thus, for 4 cuts, we have 9 pieces; for 5 cuts, we have 11 pieces; for 6 cuts, we have 13 pieces; and for 7 cuts, we have 15 pieces.

Answer: There will be 15 pieces if we make 7 vertical line cuts.

Teaching Notes: Notice that some students may recognize that the number of pieces is 2 times the number of cuts plus 1, or, algebraically, $P = 2n + 1$, where n is the number of cuts and P is the number of pieces.

Problem 7.8 (Grades 5–7)

Laura has trained her pet kangaroo, Sam, to hop up a flight of 7 steps. Sam can hop up one step at a time or two steps at a time. Sam hops up the flight a different way each time. How many different ways can Sam hop up the flight of seven steps?

Solution: We will begin with a simpler situation, building up to the required one, and searching for a pattern that might allow us to get the answer more quickly than if we were to exhaust all possibilities. We'll reduce the complexity to one step, then solve for two steps, then for three steps, and so on, and see if a pattern emerges.

Number of Steps	Ways Sam Can Hop	Number of Ways
1	1	1
2	1–1, 2	2
3	1–1–1, 2–1, 1–2	3
4	1–1–1–1, 2–1–1, 2–2	5
	1–2–1	
	1–1–2	

Aha! Each step appears to require the number of hops equal to the sum of the two previous steps (i.e., $1 + 2 = 3$, $2 + 3 = 5$). Let's try one more to see if our pattern rule is correct.

Number of Steps	Ways Sam Can Hop	Number of Ways
1	1	1
2	1–1, 2	2
3	1–1–1, 2–1, 1–2	3
4	1–1–1–1, 2–1–1, 2–2	5
	1–2–1	
	1–1–2	
5	1–1–1–1–1, 2–1–1–1, 1–2–2	8
	1–2–1–1, 2–1–2	
	1–1–2–1, 2–2–1	
	1–1–1–2	

Our pattern rule is right, and the sequence is 1, 2, 3, 5, 8, 13, 21, 34.

Rather than write the sequence, some students might simply continue the table for seven steps. This is perfectly correct and will lead to the same answer, 34. Notice, too, that this sequence of numbers is known as the Fibonacci numbers, where each is the sum of the previous two numbers. This sequence occurs in this problem because, in order to reach a given step, Sam must hop from either the step one below or the step two below.

Answer: Sam can hop up the staircase in 34 different ways.

Problem 7.9 (Grades 6–7)

David works for an art gallery. He is designing a large wall covering for a client. The entire design is made up of 50 concentric squares (squares with the same center and sides parallel). Figure 7.6 shows the first four squares of his design and gives the length of one side of each square. David is going to outline the perimeter of each square with wool. How many feet of wool does he need to outline all 50 squares?

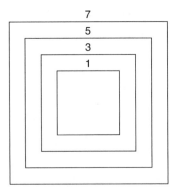

Figure 7.6

Solution: We examine the data and see if we can find a pattern to help us. Because a square has four equal sides, we can find the sum of one side of each square and then multiply by four. This will let us use smaller numbers. Starting from the smallest square and moving outward, the lengths of the sides form a sequence of the first 50 odd numbers: 1, 3, 5, 7, . . . , 99. We need to compute the sum $1 + 3 + 5 + 7 + \ldots + 99$.

$1 = \mathbf{1}$

$1 + 3 = \mathbf{4}$

$1 + 3 + 5 = \mathbf{9}$

$1 + 3 + 5 + 7 = \mathbf{16}$

$1 + 3 + 5 + 7 + 9 = \mathbf{25}$

Notice that the sums are perfect squares. In fact, each sum is the square of the number of terms being added.

$1 = 1 = \mathbf{1^2}$

$1 + 3 = 4 = \mathbf{2^2}$

$1 + 3 + 5 = 9 = \mathbf{3^2}$

$1 + 3 + 5 + 7 = 16 = \mathbf{4^2}$

$1 + 3 + 5 + 7 + 9 = 25 = \mathbf{5^2}$

Using this pattern, the sum of all 50 terms will be 50^2, or 2,500. Now we multiply by 4 to find the perimeter and arrive at 10,000 feet of wool.

You can also look at this problem from a different point of view, using a different pattern (or, if you wish, organizing data). We need to compute the sum $1 + 3 + 5 + 7 + \ldots + 99$. Instead of adding the numbers in the order in which they are written here, consider the partial sums: $1 + 99 = 100$, $3 + 97 = 100$, $5 + 95 = 100, \ldots, 49 + 51 = 100$. The total of these sums is $25 \times 100 = 2,500$. As before, we then multiply by 4 to get 10,000.

Answer: David will need 10,000 feet of wool for the wall covering.

Problem 7.10 (Grades 6–7)

When students begin the study of probability, they usually run into tree diagrams early on. In some problems, it is often helpful to make tree diagrams similar to the one in Figure 7.7.

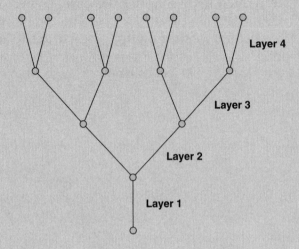

Figure 7.7

This drawing shows four layers and 15 branches in all. If we continued this drawing for 8 layers, how many branches would there be?

Solution: We could actually continue drawing the tree diagram until we had shown 8 layers. However, this would be complicated to draw and might not be very accurate. Instead, let's look for a pattern describing the relationship between the layers and branches.

Layer	Total Branches
1	1
2	3
3	7
4	15

The difference between successive numbers of branches is 2, 4, 8, . . . and continues doubling. This would make sense, because each branch emits two new ones in the next layer. Thus, we continue the table as follows:

Layer	Total Branches
1	1
2	3
3	7
4	15
5	31
6	63
7	127
8	255

Answer: There would be 255 branches in the eighth layer.

Problem 7.11 (Grades 3–4)

Lim is making a shelf for her dolls. She has 17 interlocking blocks and wants to make the largest shelf possible. If she uses 5 blocks, she can make a shelf that holds 3 dolls. Six blocks will hold 4 dolls. Seven blocks make a 5-doll shelf, and 8 blocks make an 8-doll shelf as shown in Figure 7.8. How many dolls will fit on the shelf if she continues in this manner and uses all 17 interlocking blocks?

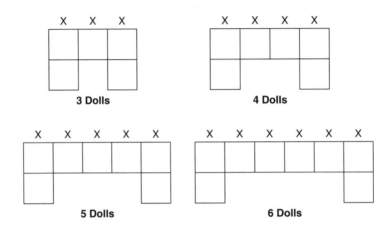

Figure 7.8

Solution: We will make a table of what we know and see if a pattern emerges.

Blocks	5	6	7	8
Dolls	3	4	5	6

The number of dolls seems to be 2 less than the number of blocks. Let's continue the table.

Blocks	5	6	7	8	. . .	15	16	17
Dolls	3	4	5	6	. . .	13	14	15

Answer: Her shelf will hold 15 dolls.

Teaching Notes: Some students may reason the problem out deductively. They see, for example, that with the exception of the two blocks forming the "legs," the remaining blocks each hold 1 doll. Thus, for 17 blocks, 2 form the legs and 15 dolls can be accommodated. This is an excellent solution with sound logical reasoning and should be discussed with the class.

Problem 7.12 (Grades 3–4)

During the World Series, one pitcher used a pattern when he pitched. The pattern was two fastballs followed by two sliders followed by a change-of-pace pitch. If the pattern continues, what kind of pitch will the 18th pitch be?

Solution: Because the pitcher pitches according to a set pattern, we can try to discover the pattern rule. The sequence he follows is F F S S C, repeating in groups of five. Thus, the 18th pitch will be a slider pitch, because there will be three groups of 5 when 15 pitches have been thrown. Therefore, three pitches later, he will have thrown his 18th pitch. The actual sequence of pitches would be:

F F S S C   F F S S C   F F S S C   F F S...

Answer: The 18th pitch would be a slider.

Teaching Notes: The emphasis in this problem is on the pattern that repeats. This happens in groups of 5. Thus, the students want to know the 3rd pitch in the 4th set of 5, which is the 18th pitch.

8

Logical Reasoning

Although solving any problem requires logical thinking or reasoning, some problems depend upon logical reasoning as the primary strategy for solving them. These can range from the simple logic of what size product yields the best price per object (i.e., the better buy) to problems that consist of a logical chain of inferences. An inference is made, which leads to a second inference, and so on. One inference leads to another. The logical process continues until the problem has been resolved.

APPLYING THE LOGICAL REASONING STRATEGY

Consider the following problem:

> Ruth, Stan, Ted, Una, Vicky, and Walt are going to dinner to celebrate Vicky's and Walt's graduation from high school. Each person's meal costs the same amount. Vicky and Walt are being treated for their own meal, but each must chip in equally for his or her share of the other's meal. How much should each person pay if the total bill was $108.00?

Solution: One of the first solutions that comes to mind is algebraic. Now

$108 \div 6 =$ a cost of $18 per meal

Let $2x$ represent the amount each person pays for Vicky and Walt. Then

Ruth pays $18 + 2x$
Stan pays $18 + 2x$
Ted pays $18 + 2x$
Una pays $18 + 2x$
Vicky pays x
Walt pays x

So

$72 + 10x = 108
$10x = 36
$x = 3.60

Vicky and Walt each paid $3.60; everyone else paid $18 + $7.20 = $25.20.
Let's try to solve this problem using **logical reasoning**. We know that Vicky paid $\frac{1}{5}$ of Walt's meal, or $\frac{1}{5}$ of $18 = $3.60. At the same time, Walt paid $\frac{1}{5}$ of Vicky's meal or $3.60, for a total of $7.20. If we subtract the $7.20 from the total bill of $108, we have $100.80 left for the remaining four people to share. Dividing $100.80 by 4, we obtain $25.20 per person, the amount paid by Ruth, Stan, Ted, and Una. Vicky and Walt each paid $3.60.

CHAPTER TEACHING NOTES

Problems involving logical reasoning often include a substantial amount of data that, at first glance, appears overwhelming and confusing. The solution strategy, as has been noted, is to draw logical conclusions from such data; that is, to use inference. However, this requires that your students learn how to sensibly and systematically organize the data. This includes learning how to analyze clues—for instance, how to use the process of elimination, lists, Venn diagrams, or matrix logic.

It is also critical that your students discuss their thinking with you and their classmates. When students are asked to solve a problem requiring logical reasoning, it is not just a matter of jumping from one fact to another. It often *requires reading between the lines.* For example, it does not say—although it can be inferred—in the above problem that Vicky pays $\frac{1}{5}$ of Walt's meal. This will be a new experience for many of your students, and they will need to discuss and explore a number of problems as they acquire the taste of efficiency and elegance that logical reasoning brings to problem solving.

PROBLEMS FOR STUDENTS

Problem 8.1 (Grades 3–4)

A man has a drawer with only black and blue socks in it. He wants to be certain he has a matching pair of socks, but it is dark in the room and he can't tell the socks apart. How many socks must he pull from the drawer to be sure he has a matching pair?

Solution: A logical approach would be to assume the worst-case scenario, namely, that he pulls out one black sock and one blue sock on his first two pulls. The third sock must guarantee that he has a matching pair.

Answer: He must draw 3 socks from the drawer.

Problem 8.2 (Grades 3–4)

Ron, Stan, Tom, and Ursula were entered in a ping-pong tournament. Ron lost to Ursula in the first-round game. Tom won one game and lost one game. Tom played Ursula in the second round. Who won the tournament?

Solution: Here we can only use logical reasoning. We begin with Tom's record. Tom won one game and lost one game. He must have won his first-round game in order to get into the second round. Ron lost to Ursula in the first round. This enabled Ursula to be in the second round. But Tom must have lost to Ursula in the second round, because he won only one game. Thus, Ursula was the tournament winner.

Answer: Ursula won the tournament.

Problem 8.3 (Grades 6–7)

Determine the values for A, B, C, and D if they are all positive whole numbers and

$A \times B = 24$
$A + B = 14$
$C \times D = 48$
$A \times D = 192$
$B \times C = 6$

Solution: Let's use some logical reasoning together with our knowledge of arithmetic. Because $A \times B = 24$, we can examine the factor pairs of 24. A and B can only be 1 and 24, 2 and 12, 3 and 8, or 4 and 6. Furthermore, because $A + B = 14$, A and B can only be 12 and 2. Notice that the last relationship, $B \times C = 6$, tells us that B must be 2 and A must be 12. Furthermore, if $B = 2$, C must be 3. Because $C \times D = 48$, D must be 16.

The logical reasoning strategy must be used by students in an open-thinking mode, and as long as students can justify their steps logically, these steps should be accepted. This can be a nice group activity.

Answer: $A = 12, B = 2, C = 3, D = 16$.

Problem 8.4 (Grades 4–6)

Mrs. Adams planted three kinds of berry plants in her garden. Of these, $\frac{1}{2}$ are blueberries, $\frac{1}{4}$ are strawberries, and the rest are raspberries. She planted 10 raspberry plants. How many berry plants did she plant altogether?

Solution: By logically reasoning what we are given and what we are asked to find, we realize that the raspberries must be the remaining quarter of the circle, since $\frac{1}{2} + \frac{1}{4} = \frac{3}{4}$. Thus, $\frac{1}{4} = 10$ raspberry plants. Therefore, the number of strawberry plants, which also represents $\frac{1}{4}$ of the plants, must also be 10. Then $\frac{1}{2}$ of the plants are blueberry, which must be 20 in number.

Answer: She planted $10 + 10 + 20 = 40$ plants altogether.

Problem 8.5 (Grades 3–5)

Draw 2 straight lines across the face of a clock (see Figure 8.1) so that the sum of the numbers in each region is the same.

Figure 8.1

Solution: A little logical reasoning should help. If we simply draw two intersecting lines to form four regions, we will be bunching the small numbers together and the large numbers together. This will be unbalanced from the start. Let's examine the problem logically. If we add all 12 numbers on the clock, we obtain $1 + 2 + 3 + 4 + 5 + 6 + 7 + 8 + 9 + 10 + 11 + 12 = 78$. Now, because the sum within each region must be the same, we divide by 3. That sum is 26. This makes the work easier. The answer is shown in Figure 8.2.

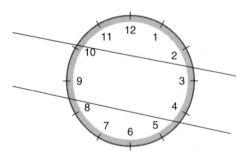

Figure 8.2

Answer: One region has $11 + 12 + 1 + 2 = 26$, another region has $10 + 9 + 3 + 4 = 26$, and a third region has $8 + 7 + 6 + 5 = 26$.

Problem 8.6 (Grades 3–4)

In the bottom of the pile of junk in the lake are a cup, a jar, a shoe, and an old tire. A fish, a frog, a crab, and a snake came along. The snake went into the jar and fell asleep. The crab crawled into the shoe. The fish won't go near the tire. Into which object did each creature go?

Solution: Make a matrix and fill in the clues. Remember, a "Yes" in any column means an "X" or a "No" in all other items in that column (up and down) and row (horizontally across). Thus, the first clue tells us that the snake went into the jar. This means a "Yes" in that cell of the matrix. It also means no one else could be in the jar (all Xs in that column), nor could the snake be anywhere else (all Xs in that row). Continue in a similar manner using the clues, one at a time.

	Cup	Jar	Shoe	Tire
Fish	Yes	X	X	X
Frog	X	X	X	Yes
Crab	X	X	Yes	X
Snake	X	Yes	X	X

The matrix shows which creature was in which object.

Answer: The fish is in the cup, the frog is in the tire, the crab is in the shoe, and the snake is in the jar.

Teaching Notes: This kind of logic problem is known as *matrix logic* because it involves drawing a rectangular matrix. It is quite popular with students, and it is one that is most often used.

Problem 8.7 (Grades 5–7)

Gene, Roberta, and Alex own a sedan, a convertible, and a sports car (but not necessarily in that order). Use the following clues to determine who owns which car.

   a. Roberta has one more child than the owner of the convertible.

   b. Alex is the brother-in-law of the sports car owner.

   c. The owner of the convertible beat Alex in ping pong.

Solution: The first clue tells us that Roberta could *not* be the owner of the convertible, Clue c tells us that Alex could *not* be the owner of the convertible. Thus, it is Gene who owns the convertible. Clue b tells us that Alex could not own the sports car. The owner of the sports car must be Roberta. This leaves the sedan for Alex.

Answer: Gene owns the convertible, Roberta owns the sports car, and Alex owns the sedan.

Problem 8.8 (Grades 4–6)

Three children, Frank, Katie, and Sherrie, are entered in the charity Bike-a-Thon. Their pledges total $2.00 per mile for each of them. Katie, the oldest, rode twice as far as Sherrie. Frank, the youngest child, rode 8 miles. Sherrie rode 5 miles more than Frank. How much money did each child earn for the charity?

Solution: We can use each of the clues in the problem to find out how many miles each child rode. Then we can find the amount each one earned for the charity. Notice that the fact that Katie is the oldest, Frank is the youngest, and Sherrie is the middle child in age has nothing to do with the problem.

The problem tells us that Frank rode 8 miles. Because Sherrie rode 5 miles more than Frank, she rode 8 + 5 = 13 miles. Katie rode twice as far as Sherrie, so she rode 13 × 2 = 26 miles. We can now find how much money each child earned:

Frank: 8 × $2.00 = $16.00
Katie: 26 × $2.00 = $52.00
Sherrie: 13 × $2.00 = $26.00

Answer: Frank earned $16.00, Katie earned $52.00, and Sherrie earned $26.00.

Problem 8.9 (Grades 5–7)

Mario went to the movies last Friday. While he was there, he bought hot popcorn (without butter) and a cold apple juice. The popcorn costs $2 plus half its price, while the juice costs $1 plus half its price. He bought one box of popcorn and one juice. What was his total cost if the tax is included?

Solution: Let's use some logical reasoning. If the popcorn costs $2 plus half its price, then the $2 must be the "other half" of the price. So, the popcorn costs $4. Similarly, the price of the juice must be $1 plus $1 or $2.

Answer: Mario spent $6 on popcorn and juice.

Problem 8.10 (Grades 5–6)

John's homework was writing large numbers that would be divisible by 3. He spilled some ink over the last digit in his number: 123,547,295,42__. What is the missing digit in John's number if it is divisible by 3?

Solution: We shall use the rule for divisibility by 3 and some logical reasoning. A number is divisible by 3 if the sum of its digits is a multiple of 3. Thus, 327 is divisible by 3 because $3 + 2 + 7 = 12$, which is divisible by 3.

If we add $1 + 2 + 3 + 5 + 4 + 7 + 2 + 9 + 5 + 4 + 2$, we get 44. Thus, the missing digit cannot be 0 because 44 is not divisible by 3. What can it be? It could be 1 (the sum of the digits would be 45) or it could be 4 (the sum would be 48) or it could be 7 (the sum would be 51). Thus, there is more than one possible correct answer.

Answer: The missing digit that was covered by ink could be 1, 4, or 7.

Problem 8.11 (Grades 4–6)

Ron, Sarah, and Theo are salespersons at the used car fair. They sold a Honda, a Toyota, and a Nissan. The person who sold the Toyota is older than Sarah. Theo sold the Nissan. Which car did each person sell?

Solution: Let's use some logical reasoning. Because the person who sold the Toyota is older than Sarah, it was not Sarah who sold the Toyota. Furthermore, because Theo sold the Nissan, Sarah could only have sold the Honda. This leaves the Toyota for Ron.

Answer: Ron sold the Toyota, Sarah sold the Honda, and Theo sold the Nissan.

Problem 8.12 (Grades 4–6)

Mrs. Ross has three children: Louis, Myra, and Howard. The sum of their ages is 34. Louis is the oldest. Myra is not the youngest. Howard is 8 years younger than the oldest who is 16 years old. How old are the three children?

Solution: We use logical reasoning. The problem tells us that Louis is the oldest and that he is 16. Myra is not the youngest, which means Howard is the youngest. This makes Howard 8 years old (8 years younger than Louis). The middle child is Myra. Because the sum of the ages of the three children is 34, we add $16 + 8 = 24$. This leaves 10 years for Myra.

Answer: Louis is 16, Myra is 10, and Howard is 8.

Problem 8.13 (Grades 6–7)

Michelle has a coin collection in three boxes. One box contains all dimes, one contains all nickels, and one contains both nickels and dimes. During a recent flood, the labels fell off and her younger brother put them all back on the boxes. However, all three boxes are now labeled incorrectly. Without looking into the boxes, Michelle took one coin from one of the boxes. She looked at the coin and said, "Now I can label the boxes correctly." How did she do it?

Solution: Take one coin from the box labeled "Nickels and Dimes." Suppose it is a nickel. Then the box cannot contain "Nickels and Dimes," so it must be labeled incorrectly. Thus, that box is "Nickels." This means the box labeled "Dimes" cannot be dimes, but must be "Nickels and Dimes." Finally, this leaves only the box labeled "Nickels" as the box containing the dimes. A similar argument can be made if the coin taken from the box labeled "Nickels and Dimes" is a dime.

Answer: The box labeled "Nickels and Dimes" contains only nickels. The box labeled "Nickels" cannot contain nickels and must contain the dimes. Thus, the box labeled "Dimes" must contain the nickels and dimes.

Teaching Notes: It may help the students if you draw three boxes and label them incorrectly as N, D, and N & D. Then, by removing one coin from the box labeled "Nickels and Dimes," we immediately relabeled that box as either all N or all D. We can cross out the original labels and continue the discussion with the remaining two drawings.

Problem 8.14 (Grades 4–6)

The Saunders family took a camping trip. The four children are sleeping in two double-decker bunk beds in the closest cabin. From youngest to oldest, the children are Maureen, Nathan, Oran, and Patricia. Nathan's younger sister is in the bed below Oran's older sister. Nathan and Oran drew lots to see who got the upper bed. Nathan lost. Where are the four children sleeping in the cabin?

Solution: We use logical reasoning. The sisters are Maureen and Patricia, and the brothers are Nathan and Oran. Nathan and Oran drew lots and Nathan lost, so Oran is in the upper bunk bed. Similarly, the problem tells us that Patricia, the younger sister, is below the older sister, Maureen.

Answer: The upper bunk beds belong to Maureen and Oran. Nathan is below Oran and Patricia is below Maureen.

Problem 8.15 (Grades 6–7)

An ad appeared in a local paper offering to sell a piece of land at $25 per square foot. The ad showed a picture of the lot (see Figure 8.3):

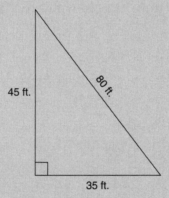

Figure 8.3

Mr. and Mrs. Adams decided to buy the plot of land and use it for a billboard for the new science museum. How much should they pay?

Solution: Let's examine the plot of land from a logical point of view. The sum of the two legs is $35 + 45 = 80$. The triangle could not exist, because the sum of any two legs of a triangle must be greater than the third leg.

Answer: They shouldn't pay anything! The plot of land does not exist!

Teaching Notes: This problem depends on a student's knowledge of the properties of a triangle. It provides an excellent problem situation in which to review the concepts of the relative lengths of the sides of a triangle.

Problem 8.16 (Grades 3–5)

The coach of the high school tennis team has to select two men and two women to join the team. Six people had tried out. But the demands of six students made it difficult for him to choose.

(1) Mitch said, "I'll play only if Sarah plays also."

(2) Sarah said, "I won't play if Ron is on the team!"

(3) Ron said, "I won't play if Dan or Emily is on the team."

(4) Dan said, "I'll play only if Amanda plays."

(5) Amanda really didn't care.

Who should he choose?

Solution: Let's see if logical reasoning makes solving this problem easier. The first statement says that Mitch and Sarah must be together. The fourth clue says that Dan and Amanda must be together. If Ron is chosen, clue three tells us that Dan and Emily are eliminated and clue two says Sarah would be eliminated if Ron were picked. So, this means that Ron cannot play, because if he did, three people would not play, leaving only three members of the team. The coach should select Mitch, Sarah, Dan, and Amanda.

Answer: The coach should choose Mitch, Sarah, Dan, and Amanda.

Problem 8.17 (Grades 4–6)

Jan was walking past the school parking lot and noticed a strange fact. All but three of the cars parked there were made by General Motors, all but three of the cars were made by Ford, all but three were made by Chrysler, and all but three were made by Nissan. What's the smallest number of cars that Jan could have seen in the parking lot?

Solution: Let's use some logical reasoning. Rather than focus our attention on what *must* be in the parking lot, look at what need not be there. There needs to be at least four cars in the lot because there is at least one car made by each manufacturer. It is not difficult to show that there need be only four cars in the lot. We need one by each of the given manufacturers. The other 3 are *not* by that manufacturer.

Answer: The minimum number of cars in the lot is 4.

Making a Drawing

To try to solve a geometric problem without drawing a diagram of the situation would be rather silly. Yet a drawing can be quite useful sometimes in solving non-geometric problems. As a matter of fact, there are times when drawing a diagram to solve a non-geometric problem is indispensable. Yet determining when a problem can be better solved with the aid of a diagram is something that comes with some practice. In this chapter, we will give you a few illustrations to begin your thinking in that direction. We will look at some problems that make use of a drawing to clarify a situation, or help the problem solver reach a satisfactory conclusion.

APPLYING THE MAKING A DRAWING STRATEGY

Consider the following problem:

> Al is holding four cards in his hand: the ace of spades, the ace of hearts, the ace of clubs, and the ace of diamonds. Steve pulls two of the cards from Al's hand without looking. What is the probability that Steve has pulled at least one black ace? (Note the clubs and the spades are the black cards.)

Solution: You might make an initial guess that the probability is 2 out of 4; that is, half the time. However, if we make a drawing of the possible outcomes, we find that this is not correct (see Figure 9.1).

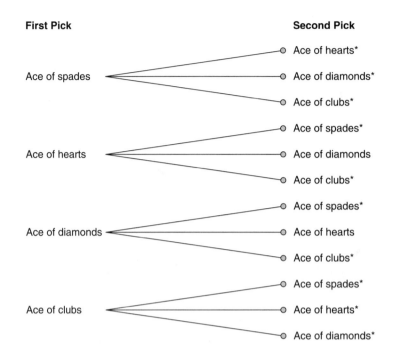

First Pick

Ace of spades

Ace of hearts

Ace of diamonds

Ace of clubs

Second Pick

Ace of hearts*
Ace of diamonds*
Ace of clubs*

Ace of spades*
Ace of diamonds
Ace of clubs*

Ace of spades*
Ace of hearts
Ace of clubs*

Ace of spades*
Ace of hearts*
Ace of diamonds*

Figure 9.1

(where * refers to a success: at least one black ace)

Our drawing quickly reveals that there are 12 possible outcomes, of which 10 are successful (that is, at least one ace drawn is black). The correct answer is $\frac{10}{12}$ or $\frac{5}{6}$ rather than $\frac{1}{2}$ initially guessed. Making a careful drawing of the situation quickly reveals the correct answer.

CHAPTER TEACHING NOTES

As noted, much of the power in a drawing lies in how it organizes and clarifies data. The old adage "A picture is worth a thousand words" does not just refer to the economy of representation, but to the very fact that there is *seeable* representation. That is, a picture, properly done, provides a meaningful explanation of the structure of a problem. As a consequence, some of your students initially may not find it easy to create such pictures. In these cases, you might recall that students often benefit from acting out a problem, and a tree diagram, as shown above in a sense, provides a schematic "acting out" representation—not a work of art—of the problem situation. It is, in a manner of speaking, a sort of shorthand, cluing students to proceed one step at a time. Thus, in discussions with and among students, you should illustrate how diagrams and pictures can be used efficiently to record possible actions and outcomes. Such discussion will support the necessary student experimentation and exploration that precedes skill in using this strategy.

PROBLEMS FOR STUDENTS

Problem 9.1 (Grades 3–5)

There are 4 rides at the school carnival: the Carousel, the Fish Ride, the Gliding Swans, and the Giant Wheel. The Gliding Swans is on the far left. The Fish Ride is between the Giant Wheel and the Carousel. The Giant Wheel is next to only one other ride. In what order are the rides from left to right?

Solution: Make a horizontal drawing in the form of an "arrangement line." Use the clues given to place the rides along this line. Begin by placing the Gliding Swans on the far left of the line. Because the Giant Wheel is next to only one other ride, it must be at the far right. The Fish Ride is between the Carousel and the Giant Wheel. The order is:

Gliding Swans	Carousel	Fish Ride	Giant Wheel

Answer: From left to right, the rides are the Gliding Swans, Carousel, Fish Ride, and Giant Wheel.

Problem 9.2 (Grades 5–7)

A snail is at the bottom of a 10-foot well. During the day, he crawls up 3 feet. But at night he slides back 2 feet. In how many days will the snail get out of the well?

Solution: Make a drawing of the well (see Figure 9.2), and carefully mark the position of the snail at the end of each night. At the end of each complete day, the snail will have progressed 1 foot. So, by the end of the first 7 complete days, he will have moved up 7 feet. On the morning of the eighth day, the snail will go 3 feet, and that will get him to the top of the well. Therefore, he required 7½ days to get out of the well.

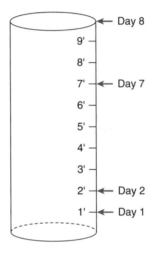

Figure 9.2

Answer: The snail will crawl out on the eighth day and will not fall back.

Problem 9.3 (Grades 3–5)

One day, five students rushed to get into the line for lunch. John was ahead of Karen and behind Leila. Leila was ahead of Sharon and behind Neville. Sharon was ahead of John. Who was last in line? Who was first?

Solution: Make a diagram of the situation being described, so that you can visualize the students' arrangement. Put the students' names into the proper positions, according to the clues given in the problem. The problem will then solve itself as you make the proper placements. Here you can see that the diagram was the only useful strategy.

FRONT OF LINE

Neville

Leila

Sharon

John

Karen

Answer: Karen was last in line and Neville was first.

Problem 9.4 (Grades 3–4)

There are 3 cacti growing in Jesse's yard. The Indian Fig cactus is 6 feet tall. The Golden Barrel cactus is 3 feet shorter than the Indian Fig cactus. The Saguaro cactus is 6 feet taller than the Golden Barrel cactus. How tall are the three cacti?

Solution: Although this problem can be solved with a bit of reasoning, many students will find it more comfortable to visualize the situation being described. We can make a drawing of the three cacti. We know the height of the Indian Fig cactus (6 feet), so begin with that one (see Figure 9.3).

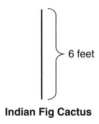

Indian Fig Cactus

Figure 9.3

The Golden Barrel cactus is 3 feet shorter, so it is 3 feet tall (see Figure 9.4).

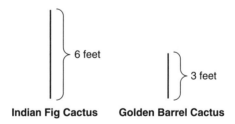

Indian Fig Cactus   Golden Barrel Cactus

Figure 9.4

The Saguaro is 6 feet taller than the Golden Barrel (see Figure 9.5).

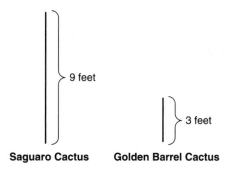

Saguaro Cactus   **Golden Barrel Cactus**

Figure 9.5

Answer: The Indian Fig cactus is 6 feet tall. The Golden Barrel cactus is 3 feet tall, and the Saguaro cactus is 9 feet tall.

Problem 9.5 (Grades 4–6)

Jenna's mom sent her to the local market. In the frozen foods section, there are only 6 items. She noticed that the chicken and hamburgers were on opposite ends of the same aisle. The waffles were across from the chicken and next to the cakes. The vegetables were on the same side as the chicken and on the opposite side from the fish. On which side of the aisle were the chicken, the hamburgers, the waffles, the vegetables, the fish, and the cakes?

Solution: Make a drawing using the clues given. We will do this piece by piece as we were given the clues. The chicken and hamburgers are on opposite ends of the same side of the aisle.

Aisle Side A	Chicken	Hamburgers
Aisle Side B		

The waffles are across from the chicken and next to the cakes.

Aisle Side A	Chicken		Hamburgers
Aisle Side B	Waffles	Cakes	

The vegetables are on the same side as the chicken. There is only one place for the vegetables, because the hamburgers and the chicken must be at the ends.

Aisle Side A	Chicken	Vegetables	Hamburgers
Aisle Side B	Waffles	Cakes	

This leaves only one spot for the fish:

Aisle Side A	Chicken	Vegetables	Hamburgers
Aisle Side B	Waffles	Cakes	Fish

Answer: The chicken, vegetables, and hamburgers are on one side of the aisle as shown. The waffles, cakes, and fish are on the other side.

Problem 9.6 (Grades 3–5)

During the summer vacation, 3 out of every 5 plants in our classroom died. We started with 40 plants. How many plants died?

Solution: A possible solution is to make a drawing of the situation. The bold slash marks represent the 3 out of 5 plants that died.

11**111**	11**111**	11**111**	11**111**	11**111**
11**111**	11**111**	11**111**		

There are 24 bold slashes out of 40.

Teaching Notes: For an older group of students, logical reasoning could provide an effective solution. By asking how many groups of 5 plants there are in 40 plants (8 groups), they then know that each group had three plants that died, or $8 \times 3 = 24$ plants died.

Answer: 24 plants died.

Problem 9.7 (Grades 5–7)

The display at the auto show consists of mountain bikes, vans, and cars. There are 18 vehicles altogether, and a total of 60 wheels. If there are four more cars than vans, how many of each are on display?

Solution: Here are the 18 vehicles (see Figure 9.6).

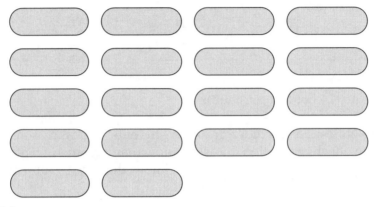

Figure 9.6

Each vehicle must have at least two wheels, so let's add two wheels to each vehicle (see Figure 9.7).

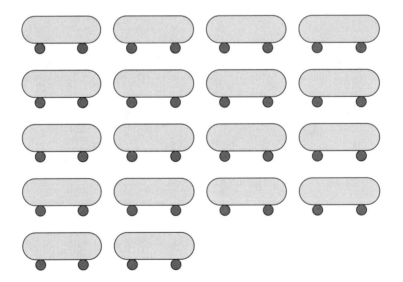

Figure 9.7

We've used up a total of 36 wheels; this leaves 60 − 36 = 24 more. They go on in pairs (see Figure 9.8):

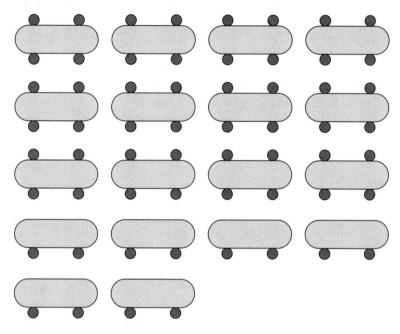

Figure 9.8

The drawing now shows that there are 12 four-wheel vehicles and 6 two-wheeled. The two-wheeled vehicles are the mountain bikes. Because there are 4 more cars than vans, there are 8 cars and 4 vans.

Answer: There are 6 mountain bikes, 8 cars, and 4 vans.

Problem 9.8 (Grades 3–5)

David is building a fence around a square-shaped garden. He puts 4 fence posts on each side. How many posts does he use?

Solution: The initial reaction of many students is to multiply 4 sides by 4 poles on each side, or 16 poles in all. However, once a drawing is made, the solution is directly at hand.

```
X   X   X   X
X           X
X           X
X   X   X   X
```

Answer: He will use 12 poles.

Problem 9.9 (Grades 4–6)

Louise wants to hang four equal sized square pictures on her wall. Her mom says it's O.K., but she has to use the absolute minimum number of tacks to hang them. Louise insists that she must put one tack in each corner of each photo. What is the smallest number of tacks Louise needs?

Solution: Once again, the initial reaction is to use 4 tacks for each picture, or 16 tacks in all. However, let's make a drawing and see what happens if we overlap the edges of the pictures (see Figure 9.9).

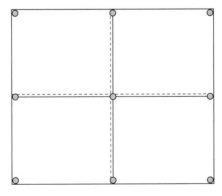

Figure 9.9

The drawing shows that she does not need 16 tacks.

Answer: Louise needs only 9 tacks to have one in each corner of each photo.

Problem 9.10 (Grades 6–7)

Arlene and her brother Mark want to start a lemonade stand after school. Together, they put in $100. Mark put in $20 more than Arlene. How much money did each of them put in?

Solution: Let's try the making a drawing strategy. Let M be the amount Mark contributes and A the amount Arlene puts into the pot. Mark put in more money than Arlene, so we shall make his rectangle bigger than hers (see Figure 9.10).

Figure 9.10

Now copy part A and place it so that its right end touches the right end of the original length A (see Figure 9.11). Then the part that isn't covered is $M - A$, which we know, is $20.

Figure 9.11

From the picture, we can see that $A + A + 20 = \$100$, so we then find that the 2 As have to equal 80, which implies that each of the As is 40.

Answer: Arlene put in $40 and Mark put in $60.

Problem 9.11 (Grades 3–4)

Ian left his house and rode his bike 8 miles due west. Then he rode 4 miles south. Next, he rode 3 miles east, then 4 miles north. How far is he from his house?

Solution: Let's make a drawing of the situation described in the problem (see Figure 9.12).

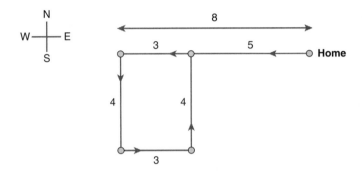

Figure 9.12

Answer: The drawing shows that Ian is exactly 5 miles from his house.

Teaching Notes: This problem is an excellent vehicle for helping the students learn about directions on a map or compass. The use of east, west, south, and north provides practice in drawing directions as they appear on a map.

Problem 9.12 (Grades 3–6)

There are 23 students in the school orchestra. There are 25 students in the band. It turns out that 7 of the students are in both. How many students are there altogether?

Solution: Let's make a drawing. We can draw a pair of overlapping circles. This is known as Euler circles or a Venn diagram (see Figure 9.13).

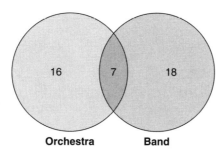

Orchestra   Band

Figure 9.13

Begin by putting the 7 students who are in *both* clubs in the region common to the two circles. This leaves 23 – 7 = 16 students in the orchestra *only*, and 25 – 7 or 18 students in the band *only*. The total number of students will be 16 + 7 + 18 = 41.

Answer: There will be 41 students involved altogether.

Problem 9.13 (Grades 3–4)

Two candles of equal height are lit at the same time. Both burn at a constant rate, but one candle takes 6 hours to burn out completely and the other takes 3 hours. After how much time will the slower burning candle be exactly twice as long as the faster burning one?

Solution: Let's make a drawing (see Figure 9.14). Candle #1 takes 6 hours, and candle #2 takes 3 hours.

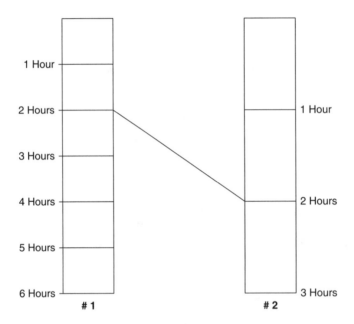

Figure 9.14

The drawing shows that candle #1 will be $\frac{2}{6}$ burned, leaving $\frac{4}{6}$ or $\frac{2}{3}$ at the end of 2 hours. During that same time, candle #1 will have burned $\frac{2}{3}$ of its length, leaving $\frac{1}{3}$ of the candle.

Answer: The slower burning candle will be twice as long after 2 hours.

Teaching Notes: This is a good time to review the concept of equivalent fractions. Thus, $\frac{2}{3}$ of the larger candle is burned down, which is equivalent to $\frac{4}{6}$ of the slower burning candle. Similarly, $\frac{2}{6} = \frac{1}{3}$.

Problem 9.14 (Grades 3–4)

Ms. Perlman has an open field that she wants to mark into separate sections. She leaves one-half of the field for her three horses. Of the rest, $\frac{2}{3}$ is marked off for the turkeys to roam freely. The remainder lies fallow for this season. How much of the field lies fallow?

Solution: Students may decide to add $\frac{1}{2} + \frac{2}{3}$ and get $\frac{7}{6}$. Obviously, this is incorrect, because $\frac{7}{6}$ is greater than one whole field. Instead, let's make a drawing to see what is going on. First, we divide the field in half (see Figure 9.15).

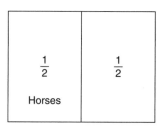

Figure 9.15

Now we mark $\frac{2}{3}$ of the remainder for the turkeys (see Figure 9.16). Notice that we are cutting only one-half of the field into three equal parts, or $\frac{3}{6}$. Two-thirds of this is for the turkeys.

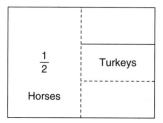

Figure 9.16

This leaves $\frac{1}{6}$ of the original field to lie fallow this year.

Answer: One-sixth of the original field lies fallow.

Teaching Notes: This problem provides you with the opportunity to make the point that fractions must be fractional parts *of something*. That is, there is no such thing as one-third. It must be one-third of something. In this case, we wanted two-thirds *of one half.* This is an important point and should be discussed with the class.

10

Adopting a Different Point of View

S ometimes, a problem can be solved in a more efficient and interesting manner if we approach it from a different point of view. That is, instead of considering the problem in the most direct and obvious manner, a different approach may yield the answer quickly and more efficiently. It also might reveal some interesting reasoning. This is not to say that the original or more obvious solution is incorrect. It is perfectly valid. However, sometimes, examining the problem from a different point of view can offer some excellent mathematics and should be discussed. Remember that most mathematical problems can be solved in a number of valid ways. Some will clearly be more elegant than others, and that might be a subject for discussion with the class. We should encourage students to use their ingenuity and then compare solutions. Learning the most elegant method might be a goal to keep in mind. There is much more to be gained by solving one problem in several ways than by solving several problems each in only one way.

APPLYING THE ADOPTING A DIFFERENT POINT OF VIEW STRATEGY

Consider the following problem

Correct to two decimal places, find the value of $3.1416 \times 2.7831 + 3.1416 \times 12.27 - 5.0531 \times 3.1416$.

Solution: The most common and obvious method for solving this problem is to find the three separate products and then add or subtract as necessary. Using a calculator, we obtain

$$
\begin{aligned}
3.1416 \times 2.7831 &= 8.743387 \\
+ 3.1416 \times 12.27 &= 38.547432 \\
&= 47.290819
\end{aligned}
$$

$$
\begin{aligned}
- 5.0531 \times 3.1416 &= 15.874818 \\
&= 31.416001 \\
&= 31.42 \text{ to the nearest hundredth.}
\end{aligned}
$$

Notice that to do all this, we needed to carefully arrange the work and keep track of the partial products. In addition, if we were using a calculator to solve the problem, it is possible that we could easily enter an incorrect digit and not even be aware of it.

Let's examine this problem from another point of view. There is a common factor in each term, namely, 3.1416. If we factor out this term, we obtain

$$
\begin{aligned}
3.1416 \times (2.7831 + 12.27 - 5.0531) &= 3.1416 \times (10) \\
&= 31.41600 \\
&= 31.42 \text{ to the nearest hundredth,} \\
&\quad \text{a much simpler procedure.}
\end{aligned}
$$

Note that this solution also involves a pattern; that is, recognizing that there is a common factor in each term. This sort of *pattern recognition* is worth highlighting.

CHAPTER TEACHING NOTES

These problems have the potential to be among the more engaging problems in this book. Your students are not so much being asked to find a solution to a problem, but to find the most elegant—and remember, we all have different tastes—and efficient solution. For this reason, it is critical that solutions be explained, illustrated, and discussed. Students are aware that there are efficient ways of solving problems, and many have experienced the glow of having found a solution to a complex problem; however, they are often unaware that mathematics has an aesthetic dimension.

Your task in helping your students to develop such an aesthetic is somewhat similar to the way in which you might help them develop an appreciation of music or art. Students need some exposure to and discussion of the elegant. They need some opportunities to explore elegance together, and they need individual opportunities to build on such discussions and exploration in their own structuring of solutions. Most importantly, they need to know that you and their peers value, appreciate, and applaud their efforts.

PROBLEMS FOR STUDENTS

Problem 10.1 (Grades 5–7)

How many towers, each consisting of 4 blocks, can be made from blocks of 2 different colors?

Solution: Rather than acting it out as we did in Chapter 5 (Problem 5.5), let's consider this problem from another point of view. Let the two colors be red and green. Each color, red or green, can be either used or not used in any position. Thus, for the first block, there are 2 possibilities, red or green. For the second block, there are 2 possibilities, red or green. Similarly, for each of the third and fourth blocks, there are two possibilities. Using the fundamental counting principle of mathematics, there are, altogether, $2 \times 2 \times 2 \times 2$ or 16 possible ways of placing the blocks.

Answer: There are 16 possible ways of making a tower of 4 blocks with two differently colored blocks.

Teaching Notes: This approach will give you an opportunity to discuss the fundamental counting principle of mathematics within the context of a problem-solving situation. The Fundamental Counting Principle states that if Task A can be performed in any one of x ways, and if, after Task A is performed, Task B can be performed in any one of y ways, then the combination tasks, A followed by B, can be performed in xy ways.

Problem 10.2 (Grades 5–7)

There are 16 children entered in the ping-pong tournament at Wagner Elementary School. The tournament is a single elimination tournament. This means that if you lose a game, you're out of the tournament. If you win a game, you move on to the next round. How many games must be played to have a winner?

Solution: If students were to use the simulation strategy, they might proceed as follows:

> In round one, the 16 players engage in 8 games. There are 8 winners to move on to the next round (8 games played). In the second round, the 8 players meet in 4 games; there are 4 winners (4 more games played). In round three, the 4 players meet in 2 games; there are 2 winners (2 more games played). In the final round, the two remaining players meet and a winner is found (1 more game played). The total number of games played is $8 + 4 + 2 + 1 = 15$.

Let's look at this problem from a different point of view. In order for there to be one winner, we must eliminate 15 other players. Because one player is eliminated each time a game is played, we must eliminate 15 players to find the champion. This requires 15 games played. The problem is easily solved following this line of reasoning.

Answer: There will be 15 games in the tournament.

Problem 10.3 (Grades 5–7)

Find the difference between the sum of all the even numbers less than 101 and the sum of all the odd numbers less than 101.

Solution: Some students may attack the problem by adding all the odd numbers less than 101, and adding all the even numbers less than 101, then finding the difference between these sums.

$$1 + 3 + 5 + 7 + \ldots + 97 + 99 = 2500$$
$$2 + 4 + 6 + \ldots + 98 + 100 = 2550$$

The difference is 50.

Let's look at this from a different point of view. We can group the numbers in pairs as follows:

$$(2 - 1) + (4 - 3) + (6 - 5) + \ldots + (100 - 99) = 1 + 1 + 1 + \ldots + 1 = 50$$

Answer: The difference is 50.

Problem 10.4 (Grade 5–7)

There are 28 comic books in Elena's collection. The comics are all either Super Hero or Comedy Hero. There are 8 more Super Hero than Comedy Hero. How many of each kind are there in Elena's collection?

Solution: Some students might use the guess and test strategy together with a table of values to help organize the data.

Comedy Hero	Super Hero	Total
5	13	18 (Too few)
6	14	20 (Still too few)
8	16	24 (Better)
10	18	28 (Yes!)

Let's consider the problem from a different point of view. Remove the 8 extra Super Hero comic books. This leaves 20 in all, of which 10 are Super Hero and 10 are Comedy Hero. Now put the 8 Super Hero comics back. Now there are 10 + 8 or 18 Super Hero comic books.

Answer: There are 18 Super Hero comic books in her collection.

Problem 10.5 (Grades 5–7)

Brunhilde threw three darts and hit the target (Figure 10.1) each time. None of the darts landed on a line. Which of the following could be Brunhilde's score?

11, 16, 17, 24, 33

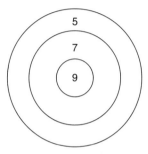

Figure 10.1

Solution: Some students might create an organized list of all the possible scores and examine them to see which scores are present. Let's examine the problem from another point of view. The numbers on the dartboard are all odd; thus, any sum of three scores will be odd. This eliminates 16 and 24. Next, we can look at the smallest possible score, namely 3×5 or 15. This eliminates 11. Similarly, the largest possible score is 3×9 or 27. This eliminates 33. The only possible score for Brunhilde was 17.

Answer: Brunhilde's score was 17.

Problem 10.6 (Grade 4–6)

There are four finalists, Al, Barbara, Carol, and Dan, who are competing for two prizes in a photo contest. In how many different ways can the first and second prizes be awarded?

Solution: One way to solve this problem is to draw a tree diagram as shown in Figure 10.2.

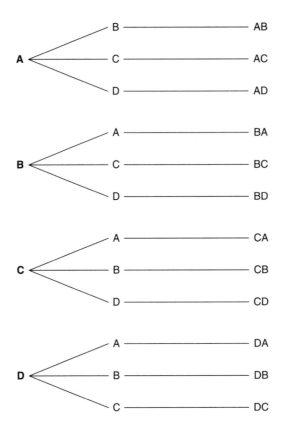

Figure 10.2

This gives the answer, 12.

Let's approach the problem from a different point of view. The first prize can be awarded to any one of the 4 people. Once it has been awarded, the next prize can be awarded to each of 3 people. Thus there are 4 × 3 or 12 ways to award the two prizes.

Problem 10.7 (Grades 6–8)

In the song "The Twelve Days of Christmas," a person receives a set of gifts each day for 12 days. On the first day, she received one gift—a partridge in a pear tree. On the second day, she receives two turtle doves and another partridge in a pear tree—a total of three new gifts. On the third day, she receives a new gift (three French hens) plus the gifts given on the second day, for a total of six new gifts. This continues for 12 days. How many gifts does she receive on the 12th day?

Solution: Students may approach the problem by making a table showing the number of gifts received each day.

First Day	$1 = 1$
Second Day	$1 + 2 = 3$
Third Day	$1 + 2 + 3 = 6$
Fourth Day	$1 + 2 + 3 + 4 = 10$
Fifth Day	$1 + 2 + 3 + 4 + 5 = 15$

They can continue in this manner until they reach Day 12.

Let's consider this from another point of view. The numbers 1, 3, 6, 10, 15 . . . are a special group of numbers known as the triangular numbers. If your students recognize them, the sequence is easy to continue. If not, arrange these numbers horizontally:

1, 3, 6, 10, 15 . . .

Now take the difference between successive terms:

1		3		6		10		15	
	2		3		4		5		6

We can now continue using these differences to arrive at the 12th number in the sequence, 78.

Answer: The person receives 78 gifts on the 12th day.

Teaching Notes: Another interesting approach is to examine the numbers in the Pascal Triangle (which may not be familiar to your students):

							1						
First						1		*1*					
Second					1		2		**1**				
Third				1		*3*		**3**		1			
Fourth			1		4		**6**		4		1		
Fifth		1		*5*		**10**		10		5		1	
Sixth	1		*6*		**15**		20		15		6		1

And so on. The bold numbers are the number of gifts each day.

Problem 10.8 (Grades 4–6)

When one rectangle is drawn, there is only one rectangle. When two rectangles are drawn end to end as shown below, there are a total of three rectangles. When three rectangles are drawn end to end, there are a total of six rectangles (see Figure 10.3). How many total rectangles are there when six rectangles are drawn end to end?

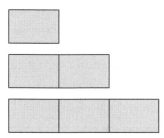

Figure 10.3

Solution: Some students might draw the rectangles consisting of four, five, and six small rectangles placed end to end, and then count the number of rectangles of different sizes (see Figure 10.4). For example,

Figure 10.4

Let's look at this from another point of view. The numbers 1, 3, 6 might be familiar. Once again, they are the beginning of the sequence known as the triangular numbers.[1] Having recognized this pattern, the next one should be 10. Let's look more closely at Figure 10.4 to see if this pattern holds true.

Single Small Rectangles	Two Rectangles	Three Rectangles	Four Rectangles	
4	3	2	1	= 10

---

1. Triangular numbers are those that represent the number of dots that can be arranged in the shape of an equilateral triangle. They are 1, 3, 6, 10, 15, . . .

The sequence holds true—it is 10. We can find the number of rectangles when six are placed end to end by continuing the sequence:

1

$1 + 2 = 3$

$1 + 2 + 3 = 6$

$1 + 2 + 3 + 4 = 10$

$1 + 2 + 3 + 4 + 5 = 15$

$1 + 2 + 3 + 4 + 5 + 6 = 21$

Answer: There are 21 rectangles of different sizes when the six rectangles are placed end to end.

Problem 10.9 (Grades 6–7)

Find the sum of the first 20 even numbers.

Solution: Some students might write the first 20 numbers out and add them. Let's try a solution from another point of view as we did in the previous problem. You will notice that with the partial sums, there is still another pattern that can be discovered by your students.

2	$= 2$	$= 1 \cdot 2$
$2 + 4$	$= 6$	$= 2 \cdot 3$
$2 + 4 + 6$	$= 12$	$= 3 \cdot 4$
$2 + 4 + 6 + 8$	$= 20$	$= 4 \cdot 5$
$2 + 4 + 6 + 8 + \ldots + 2n$		$= n(n + 1)$

Thus, for the first 20 even numbers, the sum is $20 \cdot 21 = 420$.

Answer: The sum of the first 20 even numbers is 420.

Problem 10.10 (Grades 6–7)

Find the sum of the first 20 odd numbers.

Solution: Some students might write out the first 20 odd numbers and add them:

$$1 + 3 + 5 + 7 + 9 + 11 + 13 + \ldots + 39 = 400$$

Let's approach this from a different point of view. Suppose we add the first two numbers and then the first three numbers and then the first four numbers and see if a pattern emerges.

1	$= 1$	$= 1^2$
$1 + 3$	$= 4$	$= 2^2$
$1 + 3 + 5$	$= 9$	$= 3^2$

We would then expect that for n such numbers, the sum would be

$$1 + 3 + 5 + \ldots + (2n - 1) = n^2$$

Therefore, for the first 20 odd numbers, the sum is 20^2.

Answer: The sum of the first 20 odd numbers is 400.

Problem 10.11 (Grades 5–7)

ABCD is a square with area 64 square centimeters. M and N are midpoints of their respective sides (see Figure 10.5). What is the area of the shaded portion of the picture?

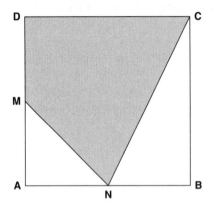

Figure 10.5

Solution: Your students may try to find the area of the shaded portion directly. They would identify each side of the square as 8, but the irregular shape of quadrilateral DMNC makes finding its area difficult.

However, let's look at the problem from a different point of view and focus on the *unshaded* part of the figure. We can make the solution simpler and, at the same time, provide students with a nice model for this strategy. Let's draw the lines connecting the midpoints of the square (see Figure 10.6).

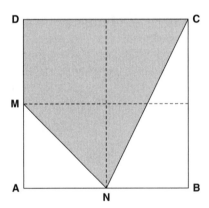

Figure 10.6

You can see that triangle AMN is $\frac{1}{8}$ (i.e., half of a quarter) of the original figure. Furthermore, triangle BCN is $\frac{1}{4}$ (i.e., half of a half) of the original figure. Therefore, the unshaded portion is $\frac{1}{4} + \frac{1}{8} = \frac{3}{8}$ of the original figure, or $\frac{3}{8}$ of 64 = 24 square centimeters. If we now subtract from the original area (60), we obtain our answer.

Answer: The shaded portion has an area of 40 square centimeters.

Problem 10.12 (Grades 5–7)

A square EFGH is formed by connecting points on the sides of square ABCD as shown in Figure 10.7. AF = BG = CH = DE = 4" and FB = CG = DH = EA = 3". What is the area of the shaded portion of the figure?

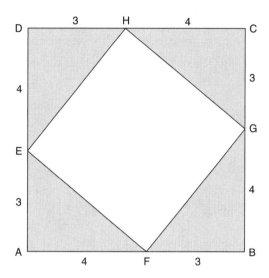

Figure 10.7

Solution: Some students may attempt to find the area of the smaller square and subtract it from the area of the larger square. However, this requires a knowledge of the Pythagorean theorem to find a side of the inner square:

$$a^2 + b^2 = c^2$$
$$3^2 + 4^2 = 9 + 16 = 25$$
$$c^2 = 25$$
$$c = 5$$

Now we can compute the two areas. The area of the larger square, $ABCD = 7 \times 7$ or 49. The area of the inner square $EFGH = 5 \times 5 = 25$. Then subtracting the two areas: $49 - 25 = 24$ square inches and the problem is solved.

Let's consider the problem from a different point of view. The shaded area is composed of four congruent right triangles each with legs 3 and 4. Thus, the area of one triangle is given by the formula $A = (1/2)(\text{leg})(\text{leg}) = (1/2)\,3 \times 4 = 6$. There are four triangles, so $4 \times 6 = 24$ square inches and the problem is solved quickly.

Answer: The area of the shaded region is 24 square inches.

Teaching Notes: Either solution is correct. Encourage your students to *discover* both.

Problem 10.13 (Grades 6–7)

Tennis balls are tightly packed with 3 in a can just touching all the sides, the top, and the bottom. Is the can's height greater than its circumference? Or is the reverse true?

Solution: Students could actually take a can of tennis balls and measure the height and distance around by using a tape measure. Let's consider the problem from a different point of view. With a drawing of the situation, we can make some observations (see Figure 10.8).

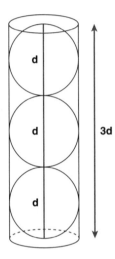

Figure 10.8

Notice that the can is exactly 3 diameters tall, or $3d$. Yet the distance around is equivalent to the circumference of a great circle through the center of a tennis ball, or πd. Because $\pi = 3.14$, the distance around is 3.14, or .14 greater than the height of the can.

Answer: The distance around the can is greater than its height.

Problem 10.14 (Grades 4–6)

In the pet shop, there is a 1,000-gallon tank that has a leak. The tank loses two gallons each day. At the end of every fourth day, an automatic timer releases five gallons of water to flow into the tank. The tank was full at the start. How many gallons will be in the tank at the end of the 20th day?

Solution: Some students may make a table to show what is taking place.

End of Day #	Out	In	Amount in Tank
—	—	—	1,000
1	2	0	998
2	2	0	996
3	2	0	994
4	2	5	997
5	2	0	995
6	2	0	993
7	2	0	991
8	2	5	994
•	•	•	•
•	•	•	•
•	•	•	•
20	2	5	985

At the end of the 20th day, there will be 985 gallons in the tank.

There is an approach that yields the answer in an efficient and elegant manner. Consider the days in blocks of 4. Every 4 days, there is a net loss of 3 gallons ($2 + 2 + 2 + 2 - 5 = 3$). Because we are interested in the 20th day, or 5 blocks of 4, we will lose 5×3 or 15 gallons.

Answer: There will be 985 gallons in the tank.

Problem 10.15 (Grades 5–7)

Marvin was counting the number of comic books in his collection. He knew he had more than 40 but fewer than 70. He put them into piles of 3 and had 1 left over. He rearranged them into piles of 4 and again had 1 left over. Finally, he rearranged them into piles of 5 and still had 1 left over. How many comic books did he have?

Solution: Some students may begin by guessing at multiples of 3, 4, and 5, and then testing their guesses. Others may try modeling the problem. However, there are other, more elegant ways of looking at this problem. For example, we can make a table showing all the numbers between 40 and 70 that fit the given conditions. Begin with more than 40 and end with fewer than 70. Be sure to count in the remainders each time.

Divisible by 3 with R1	Divisible by 4 with R1	Divisible by 5 with R1
42 + 1 = 43	40 + 1 = 41	40 + 1 = 41
45 + 1 = 46	44 + 1 = 45	45 + 1 = 46
49	49	51
52	53	56
55	57	**61**
58	**61**	66
61	65	
64	69	
67		

Even more elegant is to note that when we divide by 3, 4, or 5, we have a remainder of 1, and we can combine this division into one by the product of these three divisors, namely 60. So when we divide by 60 and get a remainder of 1, that dividend must be 61.

Answer: He had 61 comic books in his collection.

Problem 10.16 (Grades 6–7)

Given circle O with diameter AOB = 20", find the shaded area in terms of π (see Figure 10.9).

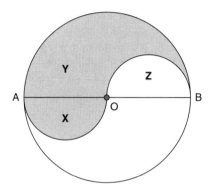

Figure 10.9

Solution: Students may attempt to find the area of the oddly shaped top part of the drawing (Y) and then add the smaller shaded semicircle (X). Let's consider this from another point of view. Because the center of the large semicircle is O, the two small semicircles have equal areas, each with diameter 10". Therefore, all we really need to find is the area of the semicircle (Y + Z). This is found with the formula Area = ½ • π • r^2 = ½ • π • 100 = 50π.

Answer: The shaded area (X + Y) = 50π.

Teaching Notes: Most of the time, unusually shaped areas are found by either adding or subtracting one or more parts. In this case, however, point out that we are merely substituting one of two congruent semicircles (X) for the other (Z).

Readings on Problem Solving

Ball, D. L. 1988. Unlearning to teach mathematics. *For The Learning of Mathematics* 8 (1): 40–48.

Brown, Stephen, and Marion I. Walter. 1990. *The art of problem posing.* 2d ed. Hillsdale, NJ: Lawrence Erlbaum.

Hoogeboom, Shirley, and Judy Goodnow. 2004. *Problem solvers II.* Chicago: Wright Group/McGraw-Hill.

Krulik, Stephen, and Jesse A. Rudnick. 1988. *Problem solving: A handbook for elementary school teachers.* Needham Heights, MA: Allyn & Bacon.

Krulik, Stephen, and Jesse A. Rudnick. 1993. *Reasoning and problem solving: A handbook for elementary school teachers.* Needham Heights, MA: Allyn & Bacon.

Krulik, Stephen, and Jesse A. Rudnick. 2000. *Teaching middle school mathematics: Activities, materials, and problems.* Needham Heights, MA: Allyn & Bacon.

Krulik, Stephen, and Jesse A. Rudnick. 2001. *Roads to reasoning (grades 3–8).* Chicago: Wright Group/McGraw-Hill.

Krulik, Stephen, Jesse A. Rudnick, and Eric Milou. 2003. *Teaching mathematics in middle school: A practical guide.* Needham Heights, MA: Allyn & Bacon.

National Council of Supervisors of Mathematics. 1977. *Position paper.* Denver, CO: National Council of Supervisors of Mathematics.

National Council of Teachers of Mathematics. 1980. *Agenda for action.* Reston, VA: National Council of Teachers of Mathematics.

National Council of Teachers of Mathematics. 1991. *Professional standards for teaching mathematics.* Reston, VA: National Council of Teachers of Mathematics.

National Council of Teachers of Mathematics. 2000. *Principles and standards for school mathematics.* Reston, VA: National Council of Teachers of Mathematics.

Polya, George. 1957. *How to solve it.* 2d ed. Princeton, NJ: Princeton University Press.

Posamentier, Alfred S., Daniel Jaye, and Stephen Krulik. 2007. *Exemplary practices for secondary math teachers.* Alexandria, VA: ASCD.

Posamentier, Alfred S., and Stephen Krulik. 2008. *Problem-solving strategies for efficient and elegant solutions—grades 6–12.* 2d ed. Thousand Oaks, CA: Corwin.

Posamentier, Alfred, and Wolfgang Schulz, eds. 1996. *The art of problem solving: A resource for the mathematics teacher.* Thousand Oaks, CA: Corwin.

Shell Centre for Mathematics Education. 1984. *Problems with patterns and numbers.* Nottingham, UK: Shell Centre & Joint Matriculation Board.

Wall, Edward, and Alfred Posamentier. 2006. *What successful math teachers do, Grades K–5.* Thousand Oaks, CA: Corwin.

CORWIN

A SAGE Company

The Corwin logo—a raven striding across an open book—represents the union of courage and learning. Corwin is committed to improving education for all learners by publishing books and other professional development resources for those serving the field of PreK–12 education. By providing practical, hands-on materials, Corwin continues to carry out the promise of its motto: **"Helping Educators Do Their Work Better."**